Contents

Gordon Moore

The Unfiltered Intel Revolution – Unauthorized

Sergei Murphy

ISBN: 9781779699947
Imprint: Telephasic Workshop
Copyright © 2024 Sergei Murphy.
All Rights Reserved.

Introduction

The Enigmatic Genius

Unearthing the Man Behind the Semiconductor Industry

Gordon Moore, a name synonymous with innovation in the semiconductor industry, is often regarded as one of the most influential figures in technology. His contributions have not only shaped the course of computing but have also laid the groundwork for the digital age we inhabit today. To truly appreciate Moore's impact, we must delve into the man himself—his motivations, his vision, and the unique blend of circumstances that propelled him to the forefront of technological advancement.

The Early Influences

Born on January 3, 1929, in San Francisco, California, Gordon Moore exhibited an insatiable curiosity from an early age. Growing up in the coastal town of Pescadero, he was surrounded by the wonders of nature, which sparked his interest in science. His childhood was marked by a fascination with chemistry, nurtured by a modest chemistry set that allowed him to conduct experiments and explore the principles of the natural world. This early exposure to scientific inquiry laid the foundation for a lifelong passion for innovation.

Moore's academic journey began at San Jose High School, where he excelled in his studies and demonstrated a keen aptitude for science and mathematics. It was here that he encountered the world of electronics, further igniting his interest in technology. The influence of World War II was palpable during this time, as the global conflict accelerated advancements in technology and engineering. This environment of rapid technological progress undoubtedly shaped Moore's aspirations and career trajectory.

1

Academic Pursuits and the Formation of Ideas

Moore's thirst for knowledge led him to the University of California, Berkeley, where he pursued a degree in chemistry. Under the guidance of Professor William Giauque, a Nobel laureate, Moore honed his analytical skills and developed a deep understanding of chemical principles. His education was not limited to chemistry; it also encompassed the burgeoning field of electronics, which would soon intersect with his work in semiconductors.

The pivotal moment in Moore's academic career came during his graduate studies when he became acquainted with the concept of the transistor. The invention of the transistor at Bell Labs in 1947 marked a turning point in the field of electronics, as it revolutionized the way electrical signals were processed and amplified. Moore's fascination with this breakthrough would later inform his work at Fairchild Semiconductor and, ultimately, Intel.

The Birth of a Visionary

In 1957, Moore co-founded Fairchild Semiconductor with Robert Noyce and a group of engineers known as the "Fairchild Eight." This venture would become a breeding ground for innovation, as it pioneered the development of integrated circuits and laid the groundwork for the semiconductor industry. Moore's keen insights and ability to foresee the potential of miniaturization and mass production set him apart as a visionary leader.

It was during this period that Moore famously formulated his eponymous law—Moore's Law—which posited that the number of transistors on a microchip would double approximately every two years, leading to exponential increases in computing power. This observation, made in 1965, was not merely a prediction; it was a clarion call for the industry to innovate relentlessly. The implications of Moore's Law extended far beyond mere numbers; it became a guiding principle for engineers and technologists, shaping the trajectory of the semiconductor industry for decades to come.

The Legacy of Innovation

As Moore transitioned from Fairchild to co-founding Intel in 1968, his vision for the future of computing continued to evolve. Intel's development of the microprocessor in the early 1970s transformed the landscape of technology, making personal computing accessible to the masses. The Intel 4004, the world's first microprocessor, was a testament to Moore's foresight and ingenuity. It was a product that encapsulated the essence of his vision: compact, powerful, and capable of performing complex calculations at unprecedented speeds.

Moore's influence extended beyond technical innovation; he fostered a culture of creativity and collaboration at Intel, encouraging his team to push the boundaries of what was possible. His management philosophy emphasized the importance of teamwork and open communication, creating an environment where ideas could flourish. This approach not only propelled Intel to the forefront of the semiconductor industry but also inspired a generation of engineers and entrepreneurs.

Conclusion: The Man Behind the Industry

In unearthing the man behind the semiconductor industry, we find a complex figure driven by curiosity, innovation, and an unwavering commitment to progress. Gordon Moore's journey from a curious child in Pescadero to a titan of technology is a testament to the power of vision and perseverance. His contributions have not only transformed the way we interact with technology but have also laid the groundwork for the future of computing. As we continue to navigate the digital landscape, Moore's legacy remains a guiding light, reminding us of the potential for innovation that lies within each of us.

The Early Years: From Chemistry to Silicon

A Curious Mind

A Childhood in Pescadero

Gordon Moore was born on January 3, 1929, in San Francisco, California, but his formative years were spent in the quaint coastal town of Pescadero. Nestled between the rugged cliffs and the vast Pacific Ocean, Pescadero was a place where nature and curiosity intertwined, shaping the mind of a future pioneer in technology. The small community, with its charming landscapes and close-knit atmosphere, provided an idyllic backdrop for Moore's early explorations and experiments.

Growing up in Pescadero, Moore was surrounded by the wonders of the natural world. The lush greenery, the sound of crashing waves, and the diverse wildlife ignited his curiosity and sparked a lifelong love for science. The simplicity of rural life allowed him the freedom to explore his surroundings, often leading him to the nearby fields and forests, where he would collect specimens and observe the intricate details of nature. This early exposure to the environment cultivated an analytical mindset, as he began to ask questions about the world around him and sought to understand the underlying principles of how things worked.

Moore's parents, both educators, played a pivotal role in nurturing his inquisitive spirit. His father, a pharmacist, and his mother, a teacher, encouraged his interests and provided him with resources to explore his curiosity. One of the most significant gifts they bestowed upon him was a chemistry set. This set would become the catalyst for many of his early experiments, allowing him to delve into the world of chemical reactions and scientific inquiry. With beakers, test tubes, and an array of colorful powders at his disposal, young Moore transformed his bedroom into a makeshift laboratory, conducting experiments that often resulted in spectacular (and sometimes messy) outcomes.

The influence of his chemistry set extended beyond mere experimentation; it instilled in him a sense of wonder and a desire to understand the principles of science. He would often conduct experiments to create colorful reactions, fascinated by the transformations that occurred before his eyes. This hands-on approach to learning laid the groundwork for his analytical thinking and problem-solving abilities, which would later prove invaluable in his career.

In addition to his scientific pursuits, Moore's childhood in Pescadero was marked by encounters with technology that would shape his future endeavors. The post-World War II era saw a surge in technological advancements, and Moore was captivated by the emerging field of electronics. He would often tinker with radios and other electronic devices, fascinated by the inner workings of these machines. This hands-on experience with technology not only enhanced his understanding of electronics but also fueled his passion for innovation.

The impact of World War II on Moore's scientific interests cannot be overstated. The war catalyzed a technological revolution, leading to significant advancements in fields such as radar, communications, and computing. As a young boy, Moore was acutely aware of the changes happening around him. He often marveled at the new inventions and the speed at which technology was evolving. This environment of rapid technological progress inspired him to dream big and envision a future where he could contribute to the field of electronics and computing.

Moore's early years in Pescadero were not without challenges. The isolation of rural life sometimes meant limited access to educational resources and opportunities. However, this adversity only fueled his determination to seek knowledge and explore the realms of science and technology. He often found solace in books, devouring literature on chemistry, physics, and mathematics. His voracious appetite for learning would become a hallmark of his character, propelling him toward academic excellence in the years to come.

In conclusion, Gordon Moore's childhood in Pescadero was a tapestry woven from the threads of curiosity, exploration, and the influence of nature. The combination of a supportive family, a passion for science, and a fascination with technology laid the foundation for his future achievements. It was in this idyllic coastal town that Moore's analytical mind began to take shape, setting the stage for a career that would revolutionize the semiconductor industry and change the course of computing history. The experiences and lessons learned during these formative years would echo throughout his life, guiding him as he ventured into the uncharted territories of technology and innovation.

The Influence of a Chemistry Set

In the quaint coastal town of Pescadero, California, young Gordon Moore's curiosity was ignited by the simple yet profound influence of a chemistry set. This seemingly innocuous collection of glass vials, powders, and instructions would serve as the foundation for a lifelong passion for science and technology. The chemistry set was not just a toy; it was a portal to the world of experimentation, discovery, and the scientific method.

The Spark of Curiosity

At a tender age, Moore was captivated by the potential of chemical reactions. The alchemy of mixing substances to create something new was a revelation. For instance, when combining baking soda and vinegar, the effervescent reaction that followed was not merely entertainment; it was a fundamental demonstration of an acid-base reaction, represented by the equation:

$$NaHCO_3(s) + CH_3COOH(aq) \rightarrow CH_3COONa(aq) + H_2O(l) + CO_2(g)$$

This early exposure to chemistry was instrumental in shaping Moore's analytical mindset. Each experiment was a lesson in observation, hypothesis, and conclusion—core principles of scientific inquiry that would later manifest in his professional endeavors.

The Role of Experimentation

Moore's chemistry set allowed him to engage in hands-on experimentation, fostering a sense of independence and problem-solving. The process of trial and error became a familiar companion, teaching him resilience in the face of failure. For instance, when an experiment did not yield the expected results, Moore learned to analyze what went wrong, a skill that would be invaluable in his future work at Intel.

The chemistry set also introduced him to the concept of controlled variables. In a classic experiment to determine the effect of temperature on the solubility of sugar in water, Moore would have learned to keep all other factors constant while varying the temperature. This foundational understanding of experimental design would later translate into the rigorous testing protocols he would advocate for in semiconductor research.

Theoretical Foundations

The influence of the chemistry set extended beyond mere experimentation; it provided a grounding in theoretical concepts. The periodic table, with its intricate relationships between elements, began to unfold before him. Understanding atomic structure, bonding, and chemical reactions was not just academic; it was a way to make sense of the world around him.

For example, the concept of moles and molarity became essential in understanding chemical concentrations. The relationship between the number of particles and the volume of solution could be expressed mathematically as:

$$C = \frac{n}{V}$$

where C is the concentration in moles per liter (M), n is the number of moles of solute, and V is the volume of solution in liters. This equation would later resonate with Moore as he navigated the complexities of semiconductor physics, where precise measurements and calculations are crucial.

Inspiration for Innovation

The chemistry set also served as a catalyst for innovation. Moore's playful experiments often led to unexpected results, sparking ideas that would later inform his work in technology. The notion of synthesizing new compounds can be likened to the process of developing new technologies—both require creativity, critical thinking, and the willingness to explore uncharted territories.

One particular experiment that left a lasting impression on Moore involved the synthesis of a simple ester, which not only produced a delightful aroma but also illustrated the concept of organic reactions. This experience exemplified how chemistry could be both a science and an art, a duality that Moore would carry into his future endeavors in technology.

Conclusion

In summary, the influence of a chemistry set on Gordon Moore's early development cannot be understated. It instilled a love for science, a methodical approach to problem-solving, and an appreciation for the intricate dance of chemical interactions. This formative experience laid the groundwork for his later achievements in the semiconductor industry, where the principles of chemistry and physics would converge to revolutionize technology. The chemistry set was not just a collection of materials; it was the birthplace of a visionary whose impact would resonate through the ages.

A Love for Science Blossoms

Gordon Moore's early fascination with science can be traced back to his childhood in Pescadero, California. Growing up in a small coastal town, the natural world surrounding him served as a vibrant backdrop for his inquisitive spirit. From a young age, Moore exhibited a keen interest in understanding the mechanisms of the world around him, a curiosity that would eventually shape his career and the very fabric of the semiconductor industry.

The Spark of Curiosity

The pivotal moment that ignited Moore's passion for science was the introduction of a chemistry set gifted to him by his father. This seemingly innocuous present opened the floodgates to a world of experimentation and discovery. Moore recalls the thrill of conducting simple experiments, mixing chemicals, and observing the reactions that ensued. It was in these formative moments that he learned the fundamental principles of chemistry—how substances interact, change, and transform.

The chemistry set not only provided hands-on experience but also instilled in Moore a sense of wonder and the importance of empirical evidence. This early exposure to scientific inquiry laid the groundwork for his analytical mindset, which would later become a hallmark of his professional achievements.

Exploring the Natural World

Moore's love for science extended beyond the confines of his chemistry set. His childhood explorations often took him outdoors, where he would collect rocks, plants, and insects, meticulously cataloging his findings. This hands-on approach to learning fostered a deep appreciation for the scientific method—a systematic way of investigating phenomena, acquiring new knowledge, or correcting and integrating previous knowledge.

As a young boy, Moore was particularly fascinated by the natural sciences. He spent countless hours observing the behavior of animals and the growth patterns of plants. This curiosity was not merely academic; it was a genuine desire to understand the principles governing life itself. Moore's early encounters with the natural world were a testament to the interconnectedness of all scientific disciplines, a theme that would resonate throughout his career.

Influence of Radio and Electronics

In addition to his chemistry experiments, Moore's interest in science was further amplified by his encounters with radio and electronics. The allure of technology captivated him, as he began to tinker with old radios and electrical components. This hands-on experience with electronics introduced him to the world of circuits, signals, and the underlying principles of communication technology.

One of the most significant projects during this period was his attempt to build a crystal radio set. The project not only required technical skills but also an understanding of wave propagation and resonance. The equation governing the frequency of a simple LC circuit, which is foundational to radio technology, is given by:

$$f = \frac{1}{2\pi\sqrt{LC}}$$

where f is the frequency, L is the inductance, and C is the capacitance. This formula encapsulates the principles of resonance, a concept that Moore would later apply in more complex systems throughout his career.

The Impact of World War II

The onset of World War II further shaped Moore's scientific interests. The war effort spurred advancements in technology and engineering, creating a fertile ground for innovation. Moore was particularly inspired by the developments in radar technology and the use of electronics in military applications. The urgency of wartime innovation showcased the profound impact that science and technology could have on society.

During this time, Moore's passion for science was not merely an academic pursuit; it became a patriotic endeavor. He recognized that scientific advancements could lead to significant societal changes, a realization that would influence his future work in the semiconductor industry. The war highlighted the importance of collaboration among scientists, engineers, and policymakers, a theme that Moore would carry into his professional life.

The Intersection of Curiosity and Education

As Moore progressed through his education, his love for science continued to flourish. At San Jose High School, he excelled in his science courses, often going above and beyond the curriculum. His teachers recognized his potential and encouraged him to pursue his interests further. This support was crucial in shaping his academic trajectory, leading him to the University of California, Berkeley, where he would delve deeper into the realms of chemistry and electronics.

At Berkeley, Moore's passion for science evolved into a more structured pursuit of knowledge. He engaged with complex theories and conducted laboratory experiments that challenged his understanding. The rigorous academic environment allowed him to explore the intersection of chemistry and electronics, ultimately paving the way for his groundbreaking work in the semiconductor industry.

Conclusion

Gordon Moore's love for science blossomed from a combination of curiosity, hands-on experimentation, and the influence of his environment. From his childhood chemistry set to his explorations of radio technology, each experience contributed to his development as a scientist and innovator. The foundational principles he learned during these formative years would not only define his career but also leave an indelible mark on the technological landscape of the modern world. His journey exemplifies how early passions can evolve into revolutionary ideas that change the course of history.

Encounters with Technology: Radio and Electronics

Gordon Moore's fascination with technology began at an early age, profoundly influenced by his encounters with radio and electronics. Growing up in Pescadero, California, during the 1930s, Moore was surrounded by an environment that encouraged curiosity and experimentation. This section explores the pivotal moments that ignited his passion for technology and set the stage for his future contributions to the semiconductor industry.

The Allure of Radio

The radio was a magical device in the 1930s, serving as a gateway to the world beyond the small coastal town of Pescadero. For young Gordon, the crackling sounds of distant voices and music were not just entertainment; they were a source of inspiration.

> "I remember listening to the radio and being captivated by the idea that sound could travel through the air. It felt like magic."

Moore's early exposure to radio sparked a desire to understand the underlying principles of how these devices worked. This curiosity led him to tinker with old radios, taking them apart to explore their components. He learned about the basic elements of radio technology, including antennas, oscillators, and amplifiers.

Basic Principles of Radio Technology

The fundamental operation of a radio can be described by the equation for the resonant frequency of a circuit:

$$f = \frac{1}{2\pi\sqrt{LC}} \tag{1}$$

where f is the resonant frequency, L is the inductance, and C is the capacitance of the circuit. This equation highlights the relationship between inductance and capacitance in determining the frequency at which the circuit resonates, allowing it to receive specific radio signals.

As he delved deeper, Moore learned about amplitude modulation (AM) and frequency modulation (FM), the two primary methods of encoding information onto carrier waves. The ability to transmit voice and music over long distances fascinated him, leading him to construct his own basic radio receiver from spare parts.

The Role of Electronics in Daily Life

In addition to radio, the burgeoning field of electronics began to permeate everyday life. Moore's family owned a small farm, and he often encountered various electrical devices that piqued his interest. From the simple light bulb to the more complex electric motors, each device represented a blend of science and practicality.

Moore's father, a businessman, had a keen interest in technology and often encouraged his son to explore the mechanics of their farm equipment. This hands-on experience with machinery further fueled Moore's analytical mindset and problem-solving skills.

Experiments and Innovations

By the time he reached high school, Moore had transformed his bedroom into a makeshift laboratory. He conducted experiments with radios, amplifiers, and other electronic components, often inviting friends to join him in exploring the wonders of technology.

One of his notable projects involved building a crystal radio set. This simple device required no external power source, relying instead on the energy of radio waves to produce sound. Moore's success in constructing the crystal radio exemplified his ability to apply theoretical knowledge to practical challenges.

The basic circuit diagram for a crystal radio is illustrated below:

The circuit typically includes an antenna, a tuning coil, a diode detector, and headphones. The antenna captures radio waves, which induce a current in the tuning coil. The diode rectifies the alternating current, allowing it to produce sound in the headphones.

Influences of World War II

The onset of World War II further accelerated Moore's interest in technology. The war effort necessitated rapid advancements in communication and electronics, leading to innovations that would shape the future of the industry.

Moore was particularly intrigued by the development of radar technology, which utilized radio waves to detect objects at a distance. The principles of radar, including the Doppler effect and signal processing, captivated his imagination and deepened his understanding of electronics.

$$f' = f \left(\frac{v + v_0}{v - v_s} \right) \tag{2}$$

In this equation, f' represents the observed frequency, f is the source frequency, v is the speed of sound, v_0 is the speed of the observer, and v_s is the speed of the source. This understanding of wave behavior would later inform Moore's work in semiconductors and microprocessors.

Conclusion

Gordon Moore's early encounters with radio and electronics were not merely hobbies; they were formative experiences that laid the groundwork for his future innovations. The combination of curiosity, hands-on experimentation, and a supportive environment fostered a deep understanding of technology that would serve him well in his career. These formative years in Pescadero were instrumental in shaping the visionary who would later co-found Intel and revolutionize the semiconductor industry.

As Moore himself reflected,

"Every little thing I did as a kid contributed to who I became as an adult. The world of radio and electronics opened my eyes to endless possibilities."

The Impact of World War II on Moore's Scientific Interests

World War II was not merely a backdrop to the life of Gordon Moore; it was a catalyst that ignited his scientific curiosity and propelled him into the world of technology and innovation. The war, with its unprecedented demands for scientific advancement, created an environment ripe for exploration and experimentation, profoundly influencing Moore's trajectory as a future pioneer in the semiconductor industry.

The Scientific Landscape During the War

The global conflict necessitated rapid advancements in technology, particularly in fields such as radar, communications, and materials science. The United States government invested heavily in research and development, leading to groundbreaking innovations that would later serve as the foundation for Moore's work. The Manhattan Project, which aimed to develop nuclear weapons, exemplified the urgency and scale of wartime scientific endeavors. This project not only showcased the importance of interdisciplinary collaboration but also highlighted the potential of scientific research to effect monumental change.

Moore, who was a teenager during the war, was deeply influenced by the scientific fervor that surrounded him. The war emphasized the importance of technology in warfare, which piqued his interest in electronics and engineering. His exposure to the technological advancements of the time, particularly in radar technology, sparked a fascination with the principles of physics and engineering that would later become integral to his career.

Personal Experiences and Influences

Growing up in Pescadero, California, Moore was not insulated from the war's impact. The small coastal town, while distant from the front lines, was influenced by the national narrative of innovation and urgency. Moore's childhood experiences, particularly his interactions with a chemistry set gifted by his father, were augmented by the scientific discourse permeating society. The chemistry set served as a gateway to experimentation, allowing him to engage with the scientific method at an early age.

Moreover, the war prompted a surge in interest in electronics, as civilians sought to contribute to the war effort. Moore's early encounters with technology, including radio and electronics, were a direct result of this societal shift. The need for communication devices and radar systems created a demand for skilled technicians and engineers, inspiring many young minds, including Moore's, to delve deeper into the field of electronics.

Educational Opportunities and the War's Legacy

The war's conclusion marked a significant shift in the educational landscape, particularly in the sciences. The G.I. Bill, enacted in 1944, provided returning veterans with access to higher education, leading to an influx of students in universities across the country. This expansion of the academic community fostered an environment of collaboration and innovation that Moore would soon become a part of.

Moore's own educational journey was profoundly shaped by this post-war landscape. He enrolled at the University of California, Berkeley, where he studied chemistry. The university was a hub of scientific research, and the legacy of wartime advancements in technology continued to influence the curriculum. Moore's education was characterized by a blend of theoretical knowledge and practical application, reflecting the needs of an industry poised for transformation.

The Birth of Semiconductor Technology

The culmination of Moore's experiences during the war and his subsequent education would lead to his pivotal role in the development of semiconductor technology. The war had accelerated the need for reliable electronic components, paving the way for innovations such as the transistor. The transistor, invented in 1947 by John Bardeen, Walter Brattain, and William Shockley at Bell Labs, would become a cornerstone of modern electronics.

Moore's analytical mind, honed during his formative years, allowed him to recognize the potential of the transistor. He would later apply this understanding to his work at Fairchild Semiconductor and Intel, where he played a crucial role in the commercialization and proliferation of semiconductor technology. The impact of World War II on Moore's scientific interests cannot be overstated; it was a defining period that shaped his worldview and set the stage for his future contributions to the tech industry.

Conclusion

In conclusion, World War II served as a pivotal moment in Gordon Moore's life, influencing his scientific interests and career path. The war's emphasis on technological advancement, coupled with personal experiences and educational opportunities, created a fertile ground for Moore's future innovations. The lessons learned during this tumultuous time would resonate throughout his career, ultimately leading to the establishment of Intel and the revolution of the semiconductor industry. Moore's story is a testament to how global events can shape individual destinies, driving innovation and progress in unexpected ways.

Education and the Pursuit of Knowledge

Life at San Jose High School

Gordon Moore's formative years at San Jose High School were pivotal in shaping his analytical mind and igniting his passion for science and technology. As he navigated the corridors of this institution, he was not just a student; he was a burgeoning scientist, a thinker, and a dreamer, eager to unravel the mysteries of the world around him.

A Hub of Curiosity

At San Jose High School, Moore was surrounded by an environment that fostered curiosity and exploration. The school, known for its strong emphasis on science and mathematics, provided a fertile ground for young minds. Here, Moore excelled in his studies, particularly in chemistry and physics, where he found himself captivated by the intricate workings of the natural world.

$$E = mc^2 \tag{3}$$

The famous equation by Albert Einstein, which relates energy (E) to mass (m) and the speed of light (c), was a cornerstone of Moore's education. It symbolized the profound connections between mass and energy, igniting a deeper interest in the principles of physics. Moore often pondered the implications of such equations, envisioning their applications in real-world scenarios.

The Chemistry Club

Moore's involvement in the Chemistry Club was a defining aspect of his high school experience. Here, he collaborated with fellow students on various experiments and projects, developing a hands-on understanding of chemical reactions and laboratory techniques. The club's activities included:

+ **Conducting Experiments:** Moore and his peers conducted experiments that demonstrated fundamental chemical principles, such as acid-base reactions and the properties of gases.

+ **Science Fairs:** Participation in science fairs allowed Moore to showcase his innovative projects, where he often received accolades for his creativity and scientific rigor.

+ **Guest Lectures:** The club frequently invited local scientists and educators to speak, providing students with insights into advanced topics and career opportunities in the sciences.

These experiences not only honed Moore's technical skills but also nurtured his ability to think critically and solve complex problems.

Mentorship and Inspiration

One of the most influential figures in Moore's high school life was his chemistry teacher, Mr. Hargrove. Known for his engaging teaching style, Mr. Hargrove inspired students to question the status quo and explore the unknown. Under his mentorship, Moore developed a keen interest in semiconductor physics, a field that would later become the cornerstone of his career.

Mr. Hargrove often encouraged students to pursue independent projects, challenging them to apply their knowledge creatively. This emphasis on exploration and innovation resonated deeply with Moore, who thrived in an environment that valued intellectual curiosity.

The Influence of Peers

Moore's peers at San Jose High School played a significant role in shaping his educational journey. He formed lasting friendships with fellow students who shared his passion for science and technology. Together, they engaged in spirited discussions about scientific theories, collaborated on projects, and inspired one another to push the boundaries of their understanding.

The camaraderie among these budding scientists created a supportive network that fueled their ambitions. They often spent weekends experimenting in makeshift laboratories, driven by a shared desire to uncover the secrets of the universe.

Extracurricular Activities

In addition to his academic pursuits, Moore was actively involved in various extracurricular activities. He participated in the school's math club, where he honed his problem-solving skills and developed a love for logical reasoning. The club often tackled challenging mathematical problems, fostering a competitive yet collaborative atmosphere.

$$P(n) = \frac{n!}{k!(n-k)!} \tag{4}$$

The binomial coefficient $P(n)$, which represents the number of ways to choose k successes in n trials, became a favorite topic of discussion. Moore enjoyed exploring the applications of combinatorial mathematics, which would later influence his work in algorithm design and computer science.

A Vision for the Future

As Moore approached graduation, he began to envision a future where technology could transform the world. His experiences at San Jose High School laid the foundation for his aspirations in the semiconductor industry. He was determined to contribute to the technological advancements that would shape the future.

In the final months of high school, Moore penned a letter to himself, outlining his goals and dreams. He expressed a desire to study at the University of California, Berkeley, where he hoped to further his knowledge in chemistry and electronics. This letter would serve as a guiding light, reminding him of the ambitions that sparked his journey into the world of technology.

Conclusion

Gordon Moore's life at San Jose High School was marked by curiosity, collaboration, and inspiration. The experiences he gained during these formative years equipped him with the skills, knowledge, and passion that would propel him into the forefront of the semiconductor revolution. As he transitioned from high school to higher education, the seeds of innovation he planted during this time would soon blossom into a legacy that continues to influence the world of technology today.

Moore's Journey to UC Berkeley

Gordon Moore's academic journey took a pivotal turn when he enrolled at the University of California, Berkeley, in the late 1940s. This institution, renowned for its rigorous academic standards and innovative research environment, was the perfect backdrop for Moore's burgeoning interest in chemistry and electronics. As a young man with an insatiable curiosity, Moore found himself immersed in a world that would shape his future and lay the groundwork for his revolutionary contributions to the semiconductor industry.

The Transition from High School to University

Moore graduated from San Jose High School in 1945, a time when the world was still reeling from the effects of World War II. The war had ignited a technological renaissance, and Moore was eager to be part of this wave of innovation. The decision to attend UC Berkeley was not merely a choice of institution; it was a strategic move to position himself at the heart of technological advancement.

At Berkeley, Moore faced the challenges typical of a first-year college student. He quickly learned the importance of time management, balancing his studies with extracurricular activities. The transition from high school to university life was marked by a steep learning curve, but Moore thrived in this new environment. He was particularly drawn to the chemistry department, where he was captivated by the intricate dance of atoms and molecules, a fascination that would inform his later work in semiconductors.

Influence of Professors and Peers

One of the defining aspects of Moore's time at Berkeley was the influence of his professors. Among them was Professor William Giauque, a Nobel Prize-winning chemist whose passion for science inspired Moore to delve deeper into the field. Giauque's emphasis on experimental work and theoretical understanding resonated with Moore, who appreciated the blend of hands-on experience and intellectual rigor.

Moore's interactions with his peers were equally significant. The collaborative spirit that permeated the campus fostered an environment where ideas could flourish. Moore found himself surrounded by like-minded individuals who shared his enthusiasm for science and technology. This camaraderie would later play a crucial role in the formation of Intel and the microprocessor revolution.

The Intersection of Chemistry and Electronics

As Moore progressed through his studies, he began to explore the intersection of chemistry and electronics, a field that was still in its infancy. The post-war period saw rapid advancements in technology, and Moore was keen to understand how chemical principles could be applied to electrical engineering. His coursework included classes in physical chemistry, where he learned about the properties of materials and their behavior under different conditions.

A pivotal moment in Moore's academic journey occurred during a lecture on semiconductors. He was introduced to the concept of doping, a process that involves adding impurities to a semiconductor to change its electrical properties. The equation governing the conductivity of semiconductors is given by:

$$\sigma = q \cdot n \cdot \mu$$

where σ is the conductivity, q is the charge of the carriers, n is the carrier concentration, and μ is the mobility of the carriers. This fundamental relationship would later underpin Moore's work in developing silicon-based transistors.

Research Opportunities and Early Experiments

During his time at Berkeley, Moore seized every opportunity to engage in research. He participated in various projects that allowed him to apply his theoretical knowledge to practical problems. One of his early experiments involved investigating the electrical properties of different materials, a task that would later inform his understanding of semiconductors.

Moore's hands-on experience in the lab was complemented by his growing interest in electronics. He began to tinker with radios and other electronic devices, honing his skills in circuit design and troubleshooting. This blend of chemistry and electronics would prove invaluable as he ventured into the world of semiconductors.

The Road Ahead: Graduate Studies and Beyond

As Moore neared the completion of his undergraduate degree, he was faced with a choice: to pursue graduate studies or enter the workforce. Encouraged by his professors and motivated by his passion for research, he opted for graduate school. Moore's decision to continue his education would ultimately lead him to Stanford University, where he would further explore the realms of chemistry and electrical engineering.

In conclusion, Gordon Moore's journey to UC Berkeley was marked by intellectual growth, collaborative learning, and a burgeoning interest in the fields that would define his career. The experiences he gained during this formative period laid the groundwork for his later achievements in the semiconductor industry and his pivotal role in shaping the future of technology.

The Crucial Role of Prof. William Giauque

Gordon Moore's academic journey at the University of California, Berkeley, was profoundly influenced by the remarkable mentorship of Professor William Giauque. A distinguished chemist and Nobel laureate, Giauque's contributions to the field of physical chemistry were pivotal in shaping Moore's analytical skills and scientific outlook.

The Mentor and His Influence

Professor Giauque was known for his innovative teaching methods and deep commitment to student success. His approach to education was not merely about imparting knowledge; it involved igniting a passion for inquiry and exploration. Giauque's enthusiasm for the subject matter was infectious, inspiring students to delve deeper into the complexities of chemistry.

In the classroom, Giauque emphasized the importance of experimental evidence in scientific inquiry. He often stated, "Theory without experimentation is like a ship without a sail." This philosophy resonated with Moore, who would later apply this principle in his own research and development work at Intel.

Thermodynamics and Its Impact

One of the key areas of focus during Moore's time under Giauque was thermodynamics, particularly the third law of thermodynamics, which states that as the temperature approaches absolute zero, the entropy of a perfect crystal approaches zero. This principle is mathematically represented as:

$$S(0) = 0 \tag{5}$$

where S is the entropy and 0 represents absolute zero temperature. Giauque's research in low-temperature physics and thermodynamics laid the groundwork for understanding phase transitions and material properties, which would later be crucial in semiconductor technology.

Moore's grasp of these concepts would prove invaluable as he navigated the complexities of silicon-based technology. The ability to understand material properties at various temperatures allowed Moore to innovate in the design and manufacturing of semiconductors, which operate under a range of thermal conditions.

Research Opportunities

Under Giauque's guidance, Moore was encouraged to engage in research projects that would challenge his intellect and enhance his experimental skills. One significant project involved studying the behavior of gases at low temperatures, which required meticulous attention to detail and a strong foundation in both theory and practice.

This research experience not only honed Moore's technical skills but also instilled in him a rigorous scientific methodology. He learned the importance of hypothesis testing, data collection, and analysis, which would become the hallmark of his future endeavors in technology development.

The Legacy of Giauque's Teaching

The impact of Professor Giauque on Moore's career extended beyond the classroom and laboratory. Giauque's emphasis on ethical scientific practice and the responsibility of scientists to contribute positively to society resonated deeply with Moore. This sense of responsibility would later manifest in Moore's philanthropic efforts and his commitment to environmental sustainability through the Gordon and Betty Moore Foundation.

Moore often reflected on Giauque's influence, stating, "He taught us that science is not just about discovery; it's about making the world a better place." This ethos guided Moore throughout his career, particularly as he faced the ethical dilemmas associated with the rapid advancements in technology.

Conclusion

In summary, the mentorship of Professor William Giauque was a cornerstone of Gordon Moore's academic development. Giauque's innovative teaching, focus on thermodynamics, and commitment to ethical science equipped Moore with the tools necessary to navigate the complexities of the semiconductor industry. The lessons learned during this formative period would shape not only Moore's technical prowess but also his vision for a responsible and innovative future in technology.

As Moore transitioned from academia to industry, the foundational principles instilled by Giauque remained a guiding force in his career, ultimately contributing to the unfiltered Intel revolution that transformed the computing landscape.

Exploring Chemistry and its Intersection with Electronics

The intersection of chemistry and electronics has fueled innovations that have transformed technology as we know it. Gordon Moore, with his profound understanding of both fields, exemplified how the principles of chemistry could be harnessed to create groundbreaking electronic devices. This section delves into the pivotal moments where chemistry and electronics converged, shaping the future of the semiconductor industry.

The Role of Materials Science

At the heart of electronics lies materials science, a discipline that explores the properties and applications of various materials. The semiconductor, a material that can conduct electricity under certain conditions, is a prime example of this intersection. The development of semiconductors such as silicon (Si) and germanium (Ge) revolutionized electronics, enabling the creation of transistors, diodes, and eventually integrated circuits.

Semiconductor Fundamentals   A semiconductor is characterized by its electrical conductivity, which falls between that of a conductor and an insulator. The behavior of semiconductors can be described by the equation:

$$\sigma = nq\mu \tag{6}$$

where:

+ σ is the electrical conductivity,

+ n is the charge carrier concentration (number of charge carriers per unit volume),

+ q is the charge of an electron (1.6×10^{-19} coulombs), and

+ μ is the mobility of charge carriers, which indicates how quickly they can move through the material in response to an electric field.

The ability to manipulate the conductivity of semiconductors through doping—adding impurities to alter their electrical properties—has been a cornerstone of electronic device fabrication. For instance, adding phosphorus (P) to silicon creates an n-type semiconductor, while adding boron (B) creates a p-type semiconductor.

Chemical Processes in Electronics Manufacturing

The production of electronic components involves various chemical processes, including oxidation, etching, and deposition. These processes are crucial for creating the intricate structures found in modern electronic devices.

Oxidation and Etching   Oxidation is often used to create a silicon dioxide (SiO_2) layer on silicon wafers, which acts as an insulator and a protective barrier. The chemical reaction can be represented as:

$$Si + O_2 \rightarrow SiO_2 \tag{7}$$

Etching, on the other hand, is used to remove layers of material to create patterns on the semiconductor surface. This process can be achieved through wet etching, which uses chemical solutions, or dry etching, which utilizes plasma.

The Birth of the Transistor

The invention of the transistor in 1947 at Bell Labs marked a significant milestone in the fusion of chemistry and electronics. The transistor operates on the principles of semiconductor physics and relies on the manipulation of charge carriers. The basic structure of a transistor can be modeled using the junction theory, where two types of semiconductors (p-type and n-type) are joined together, forming a p-n junction.

Transistor Operation   The operation of a bipolar junction transistor (BJT) can be described by the following current equations:

$$I_C = \beta I_B \tag{8}$$

$$I_E = I_C + I_B \tag{9}$$

where:

+ I_C is the collector current,

+ I_B is the base current,

+ I_E is the emitter current, and

+ β is the current gain of the transistor.

These equations illustrate how a small input current at the base can control a larger current flowing from collector to emitter, exemplifying the transistor's amplification capability.

The Integration of Chemistry in Circuit Design

As electronic devices became more complex, the integration of chemistry into circuit design became increasingly important. The development of integrated circuits (ICs) required an understanding of both chemical properties and electronic behavior.

Chemical Vapor Deposition (CVD)   One of the key techniques used in the fabrication of ICs is chemical vapor deposition (CVD). This process involves the chemical reaction of gaseous precursors to form solid materials on a substrate. The general reaction can be represented as:

$$Gas_1 + Gas_2 \rightarrow Solid + By\text{-products} \tag{10}$$

CVD allows for the precise control of film thickness and composition, enabling the creation of complex microelectronic structures.

Case Study: Silicon and Its Alloys

Silicon, the most widely used semiconductor material, has unique properties that make it ideal for electronic applications. Its crystalline structure allows for efficient charge carrier movement, while its abundance and relatively low cost make it a practical choice for manufacturers.

Silicon Alloys   In some applications, silicon is alloyed with other elements to enhance its properties. For example, silicon-germanium (SiGe) alloys exhibit improved electron mobility, making them suitable for high-speed applications. The alloy composition can be tailored to achieve specific electrical characteristics, demonstrating the importance of chemistry in electronics.

Conclusion

The exploration of chemistry and its intersection with electronics has not only shaped Gordon Moore's career but has also laid the foundation for the modern technology landscape. By understanding the chemical principles that govern semiconductor behavior and processing techniques, Moore and his contemporaries were able to push the boundaries of what was possible in electronics. This synergy between chemistry and electronics continues to drive innovation, ensuring that the legacy of pioneers like Moore endures in the ever-evolving world of technology.

The Formation of Moore's Analytical Mind

Gordon Moore's analytical mind was not merely a product of his education; it was a culmination of experiences, influences, and innate curiosity that shaped his approach to problem-solving and innovation. This section delves into the pivotal moments and intellectual encounters that honed Moore's analytical capabilities, paving the way for his future contributions to the semiconductor industry.

The Role of Curiosity and Experimentation

From an early age, Moore exhibited a profound curiosity about the world around him. This inquisitiveness was nurtured by his childhood experiences in Pescadero, where he had access to nature and the tools of science. One of the most significant influences on his analytical development was his chemistry set, a gift that ignited his passion for experimentation. The ability to conduct experiments and witness chemical reactions firsthand allowed Moore to grasp the scientific method intuitively. He learned to formulate hypotheses, conduct tests, and analyze results, laying the groundwork for his analytical thinking.

Influence of Education

Moore's education played a crucial role in shaping his analytical mind. At San Jose High School, he was exposed to a rigorous curriculum that emphasized critical thinking and problem-solving. His teachers recognized his potential and encouraged him to delve deeper into the subjects he loved, particularly chemistry and mathematics. This encouragement was pivotal; it not only reinforced his love for science but also instilled a sense of confidence in his analytical abilities.

At the University of California, Berkeley, Moore's analytical skills were further refined. Here, he encountered complex concepts in chemistry and physics that required a sophisticated understanding of mathematical principles. For instance, he learned to apply the principles of thermodynamics and quantum mechanics to real-world problems, developing a keen ability to analyze systems and predict outcomes. The rigorous coursework and collaborative environment at Berkeley fostered a culture of inquiry that was instrumental in honing Moore's analytical prowess.

Mentorship and Intellectual Influences

One of the most significant figures in Moore's academic journey was Professor William Giauque, a Nobel laureate known for his work in physical chemistry. Giauque's mentorship provided Moore with invaluable insights into the nature of scientific inquiry. Under Giauque's guidance, Moore learned to approach problems systematically, breaking them down into manageable components. This analytical framework became a cornerstone of Moore's thinking, influencing his approach to both scientific research and business strategy.

Giauque's emphasis on the importance of empirical data and reproducibility resonated deeply with Moore. He understood that in order to innovate, one must rigorously test ideas and validate them through experimentation. This philosophy would later manifest in Moore's leadership style at Intel, where data-driven decision-making became a hallmark of the company's culture.

Practical Applications and Problem-Solving

As Moore transitioned from academia to the professional world, he encountered a myriad of challenges that required his analytical skills. At Bell Labs, he was involved in groundbreaking research that led to the development of the transistor. This experience not only solidified his technical expertise but also provided him with practical applications of his analytical training.

For example, during the development of the transistor, Moore faced the challenge of optimizing semiconductor materials to enhance performance. He applied his analytical skills to evaluate different materials, conducting experiments to assess their electrical properties. The ability to analyze data and draw meaningful conclusions from experimental results was crucial in this process. Moore's analytical mind allowed him to identify patterns and correlations, leading to innovations that would revolutionize the electronics industry.

The Impact of Analytical Thinking on Innovation

Moore's analytical mind was not confined to technical challenges; it also extended to strategic thinking within the business realm. As he co-founded Intel with

Robert Noyce, Moore's ability to analyze market trends and technological advancements became instrumental in shaping the company's direction. He recognized the potential of microprocessors early on and leveraged his analytical skills to develop a roadmap for Intel's growth.

One of the key equations that would later define Moore's contributions to the industry was his observation regarding the doubling of transistors on a chip approximately every two years, now famously known as **Moore's Law.** This empirical observation was not merely a reflection of technological progress; it was a testament to Moore's analytical thinking. By recognizing the exponential growth of technology, he was able to anticipate future trends and position Intel as a leader in the semiconductor industry.

$$N(t) = N_0 \cdot 2^{\frac{t}{T_d}}$$

where:

+ $N(t)$ is the number of transistors at time t,

+ N_0 is the initial number of transistors,

+ T_d is the doubling time (approximately every two years).

This equation encapsulates the essence of Moore's analytical approach—using data to predict future developments and drive innovation.

Conclusion

In summary, the formation of Gordon Moore's analytical mind was a multifaceted process influenced by curiosity, education, mentorship, and practical experiences. His ability to analyze complex problems, coupled with a systematic approach to experimentation and data interpretation, laid the foundation for his remarkable contributions to the semiconductor industry. As we explore the subsequent sections of this biography, it becomes evident that Moore's analytical thinking was not only pivotal to his success but also a driving force behind the technological revolution that reshaped the world.

Shaping the Future: The Birth of the Transistor

The Impact of Bell Labs

Bell Labs, officially known as Bell Telephone Laboratories, was a research and development subsidiary of AT&T and is widely regarded as one of the most influential institutions in the history of technology. Established in the early 20th century, Bell Labs became a crucible for innovation, producing groundbreaking discoveries that shaped the modern world. The impact of Bell Labs on the semiconductor industry and, more specifically, on Gordon Moore's career cannot be overstated.

A Hotbed of Innovation

At the heart of Bell Labs' success was its unique environment that fostered collaboration among some of the brightest minds in science and engineering. The institution was home to a diverse group of researchers, including physicists, chemists, and engineers, who worked together on projects that pushed the boundaries of technology. This multidisciplinary approach was crucial in the development of the transistor, which would later revolutionize the semiconductor industry.

The transistor, invented in 1947 by John Bardeen, Walter Brattain, and William Shockley, was a pivotal moment in electronics. Unlike vacuum tubes, transistors were smaller, more efficient, and more reliable. The ability to amplify electrical signals with transistors laid the groundwork for the development of integrated circuits, which in turn enabled the miniaturization of electronic devices. Moore's work in semiconductors would later build upon these foundational principles.

Theoretical Foundations

The theoretical underpinnings of semiconductor physics were extensively explored at Bell Labs. Researchers delved into the properties of materials and the behavior of electrons in semiconductors, which led to the formulation of key principles that govern modern electronics. The relationship between current (I), voltage (V), and resistance (R) is encapsulated in Ohm's Law:

$$I = \frac{V}{R} \tag{11}$$

This fundamental equation is critical for understanding how electrical components interact within a circuit. Additionally, the development of the p-n junction, a semiconductor device formed by the contact of p-type and n-type materials, was instrumental in the creation of diodes and transistors.

Challenges and Breakthroughs

The journey to perfecting the transistor was not without its challenges. Researchers at Bell Labs faced numerous technical hurdles, including material imperfections and limitations in manufacturing processes. However, their perseverance led to significant breakthroughs, such as the refinement of doping techniques, which allowed for the precise control of semiconductor properties.

One notable example is the work of Shockley, who proposed the idea of a three-layer transistor, which would eventually lead to the development of the silicon transistor. The use of silicon as a semiconductor material became a game-changer, as it is abundant, inexpensive, and has excellent electronic properties. The equation governing the behavior of charge carriers in semiconductors, known as the drift-diffusion equation, can be expressed as:

$$J = q(n\mu_n E + p\mu_p E) \tag{12}$$

Where: - J is the current density, - q is the charge of an electron, - n and p are the concentrations of electrons and holes, - μ_n and μ_p are the mobilities of electrons and holes, - E is the electric field.

This equation highlights the importance of both electron and hole conduction in semiconductor devices, illustrating the complexity and elegance of semiconductor physics that researchers at Bell Labs mastered.

Legacy and Influence on Moore

The legacy of Bell Labs extends far beyond the invention of the transistor. The institution's culture of innovation and collaboration had a profound influence on Gordon Moore and his contemporaries. As Moore transitioned from academia to industry, the principles and techniques he learned during his time at Bell Labs became integral to his work at Fairchild Semiconductor and later at Intel.

Moore's understanding of semiconductor physics, coupled with the innovative spirit fostered at Bell Labs, enabled him to envision the future of computing. His prediction, known as Moore's Law, articulated the exponential growth of transistor density on integrated circuits, which has driven the rapid advancement of technology over the decades.

In summary, the impact of Bell Labs on the semiconductor industry and on Gordon Moore's career is a testament to the power of collaboration and innovation. The breakthroughs achieved at Bell Labs laid the groundwork for the modern electronics revolution, shaping the trajectory of technology and establishing a legacy that continues to influence the field today.

The Experiments of William Shockley

William Shockley, a pivotal figure in the development of semiconductor technology, is best known for his role in the invention of the transistor at Bell Labs in the late 1940s. His experiments not only laid the groundwork for modern electronics but also shaped the trajectory of the semiconductor industry, influencing the careers of many, including Gordon Moore.

The Birth of the Transistor

In 1947, Shockley, along with John Bardeen and Walter Brattain, successfully demonstrated the first point-contact transistor, which marked a revolutionary advancement in electronics. The transistor, a semiconductor device used to amplify or switch electronic signals, replaced vacuum tubes and paved the way for smaller, more efficient electronic devices. The operation of the transistor is based on the principles of semiconductor physics, particularly the behavior of electrons and holes within a semiconductor material.

The basic structure of a transistor consists of three layers of semiconductor material, typically silicon, with varying doping levels. The two most common types of transistors are bipolar junction transistors (BJTs) and field-effect transistors (FETs). The BJT operates by using current to control the flow of electrons, while the FET uses an electric field.

The mathematical representation of the transistor's operation can be described by the Shockley equation:

$$I_C = I_S \left(e^{\frac{V_{BE}}{V_T}} - 1 \right) \tag{13}$$

where:

+ I_C is the collector current,

+ I_S is the saturation current,

+ V_{BE} is the base-emitter voltage, and

+ V_T is the thermal voltage, approximately 26 mV at room temperature.

This equation illustrates how small changes in voltage can lead to significant changes in current, a principle that is foundational to transistor operation.

Shockley's Work on Silicon and Doping Techniques

Shockley's subsequent experiments focused on enhancing the performance of transistors by exploring different semiconductor materials and doping techniques. He recognized that the electrical properties of semiconductors could be significantly altered by introducing impurities, a process known as doping. By adding specific elements to silicon, such as phosphorus (n-type doping) or boron (p-type doping), Shockley could control the density of charge carriers, thereby optimizing the transistor's performance.

The relationship between the doping concentration and the electrical conductivity of a semiconductor can be expressed as:

$$\sigma = q(n + p) \tag{14}$$

where:

+ σ is the electrical conductivity,

+ q is the charge of an electron,

+ n is the concentration of electrons in n-type material, and

+ p is the concentration of holes in p-type material.

Shockley's experiments demonstrated that by carefully controlling the doping levels, one could create transistors with specific electrical characteristics tailored for various applications.

The Shockley Diode and Its Implications

In the early 1950s, Shockley introduced the Shockley diode, a four-layer semiconductor device that exhibited unique characteristics. The Shockley diode could be used for switching and amplification, showcasing the versatility of semiconductor devices. The device operated based on the principle of negative resistance, where an increase in voltage across the diode led to a decrease in current, a phenomenon that could be exploited in various electronic applications.

The voltage-current characteristics of the Shockley diode can be represented graphically, illustrating the regions of operation, including the forward-biased and reverse-biased conditions. This behavior was crucial for understanding the potential applications of semiconductor devices in oscillators and amplifiers.

Challenges and Controversies

Despite his groundbreaking work, Shockley's career was not without controversy. His management style and personal beliefs often sparked debates within the scientific community. He was known for his strong opinions on eugenics and intelligence, which overshadowed some of his scientific contributions and led to a decline in his reputation.

Moreover, the competitive atmosphere at Bell Labs, combined with Shockley's insistence on maintaining control over his research, created friction with his colleagues. This environment ultimately led to the departure of several key figures, including Robert Noyce and Gordon Moore, who would later go on to found Intel and further revolutionize the semiconductor industry.

Conclusion

William Shockley's experiments and innovations in semiconductor technology were instrumental in laying the foundation for the modern electronics industry. His work on transistors and doping techniques not only advanced the field of semiconductor physics but also inspired a generation of engineers and scientists. Despite the controversies that surrounded him, Shockley's legacy remains a testament to the transformative power of innovation in technology, and his contributions continue to influence the trajectory of the semiconductor industry today.

The Trajectory of Silicon Transistors

The development of silicon transistors marked a pivotal moment in the history of electronics, transforming the landscape of technology and laying the groundwork for modern computing. This section explores the trajectory of silicon transistors, their underlying principles, and their profound impact on the semiconductor industry.

The Basics of Transistor Operation

At its core, a transistor is a semiconductor device that can amplify or switch electronic signals. The fundamental operation of a transistor relies on the movement of charge carriers, which can be electrons or holes. Silicon, a group IV element, serves as the primary material for transistors due to its favorable electrical properties and abundance.

The two main types of transistors are Bipolar Junction Transistors (BJTs) and Field Effect Transistors (FETs). The operation of these transistors can be described using the following equations:

Bipolar Junction Transistor (BJT) A BJT consists of three layers of semiconductor material, forming two pn junctions. The current through the collector-emitter path is controlled by the base current, described by the equation:

$$I_C = \beta I_B \tag{15}$$

where I_C is the collector current, I_B is the base current, and β is the current gain of the transistor.

Field Effect Transistor (FET) In contrast, a FET controls the flow of current using an electric field. The most common type, the Metal-Oxide-Semiconductor FET (MOSFET), operates based on the voltage applied to the gate terminal. The drain current I_D can be expressed as:

$$I_D = k \left((V_{GS} - V_{th})V_{DS} - \frac{V_{DS}^2}{2} \right) \tag{16}$$

where V_{GS} is the gate-source voltage, V_{DS} is the drain-source voltage, V_{th} is the threshold voltage, and k is a constant that depends on the device characteristics.

The Rise of Silicon Transistors

The journey of silicon transistors began in the late 1940s with the invention of the first transistor at Bell Labs. The initial devices were made from germanium, but as the technology evolved, silicon became the material of choice due to its superior thermal stability and performance characteristics.

In 1954, the first silicon transistor was commercially produced by Texas Instruments, marking the beginning of a new era in electronics. The transition to silicon allowed for the miniaturization of components and the integration of multiple transistors onto a single chip, leading to the development of integrated circuits (ICs).

The Impact of Moore's Law

Gordon Moore, co-founder of Intel, famously predicted in 1965 that the number of transistors on a microchip would double approximately every two years. This observation, known as Moore's Law, has driven the semiconductor industry to continually innovate and push the limits of technology.

The exponential growth in transistor density has resulted in significant improvements in computing power and efficiency. For instance, the Intel 4004, released in 1971, contained approximately 2,300 transistors, while the Intel Core i9-11900K, launched in 2021, boasts over 19 million transistors. This dramatic increase exemplifies the trajectory of silicon transistors and their role in shaping the modern computing landscape.

Challenges and Innovations

As silicon transistors have evolved, several challenges have emerged. The miniaturization of transistors has led to issues such as heat dissipation, leakage currents, and quantum effects that threaten to hinder further advancements. To address these challenges, researchers have explored various innovations, including:

FinFET Technology   FinFETs, or Fin Field-Effect Transistors, are a type of 3D transistor that provides better control over the channel, reducing leakage current and improving performance. This technology has become a standard in manufacturing advanced chips, allowing for continued scaling of transistor sizes.

Material Alternatives   In addition to silicon, researchers are investigating alternative materials, such as graphene and transition metal dichalcogenides (TMDs), which may offer superior electrical properties and enable further miniaturization.

Conclusion: The Future of Silicon Transistors

The trajectory of silicon transistors has been characterized by remarkable innovation and transformation. From their humble beginnings to the backbone of modern electronics, silicon transistors have revolutionized the way we live and work. As we look to the future, the ongoing pursuit of smaller, faster, and more efficient transistors will undoubtedly continue to shape the technological landscape for years to come.

In summary, the evolution of silicon transistors is not just a story of technological advancement; it is a testament to human ingenuity and the relentless drive to push the boundaries of what is possible in the realm of electronics.

The Role of Bell Labs' Researchers in Moore's Career

Gordon Moore's journey into the heart of the semiconductor revolution was profoundly influenced by the groundbreaking research conducted at Bell Laboratories, often referred to simply as Bell Labs. Established in the early 20th century, Bell Labs became a beacon of innovation, producing an astonishing array of technologies that would shape the modern world. This section explores how the researchers at Bell Labs played a pivotal role in Moore's development as a scientist and a leader in the tech industry.

The Legacy of Innovation at Bell Labs

Bell Labs was home to some of the most brilliant minds in science and engineering, including John Bardeen, Walter Brattain, and William Shockley, who together invented the transistor in 1947. This invention marked a watershed moment in electronics, enabling the miniaturization of circuits and paving the way for modern computing. Moore, who was deeply influenced by these developments, recognized early on the potential of transistors to revolutionize technology.

$$I = I_0 \left(e^{\frac{qV}{kT}} - 1 \right) \tag{17}$$

This equation, known as the Shockley diode equation, describes the current through a diode as a function of the voltage across it. Understanding such foundational principles was crucial for Moore as he navigated the complexities of semiconductor technology. The transistor's ability to amplify electrical signals became a cornerstone of Moore's work, leading to the development of integrated circuits that would transform the landscape of electronics.

Moore's Exposure to Cutting-Edge Research

During his formative years, Moore was exposed to the cutting-edge research emanating from Bell Labs, which was not only a hub for technological advancement but also a nurturing ground for scientific inquiry. The collaborative environment fostered by Bell Labs encouraged researchers to push the boundaries of what was possible. This atmosphere of innovation inspired Moore to think critically about the applications of semiconductor technology.

Moore's education at the University of California, Berkeley, coincided with a period when Bell Labs was making significant strides in semiconductor research. His interactions with faculty members who had connections to Bell Labs enriched his understanding of the field. This intellectual exchange was instrumental in shaping Moore's analytical mindset, allowing him to synthesize knowledge from various disciplines, including physics, chemistry, and engineering.

Collaboration and Mentorship

The collaborative spirit at Bell Labs was a defining feature of Moore's early career. The researchers there were not only colleagues but also mentors who shared their insights and experiences. Moore's admiration for the work of Shockley and others led him to seek opportunities that would allow him to engage with this innovative community.

In 1956, after completing his Ph.D. in chemistry, Moore joined Fairchild Semiconductor, a company that was founded by former Bell Labs employees. This transition was significant, as it allowed him to apply the theoretical knowledge he had gained to practical applications in semiconductor manufacturing. At Fairchild, he worked alongside some of the industry's leading figures, further solidifying the foundational principles he had absorbed from Bell Labs.

The Influence of Research Culture on Moore's Philosophy

The culture of research at Bell Labs emphasized creativity, experimentation, and interdisciplinary collaboration. This environment resonated with Moore's own philosophy regarding innovation and leadership. He believed that fostering a culture of creativity within a company was essential for driving technological advancement.

Moore's Law, which he famously articulated in 1965, can be seen as a reflection of the spirit of innovation that he absorbed during his time influenced by Bell Labs. He observed that the number of transistors on a microchip doubled approximately every two years, leading to exponential growth in computing power. This observation not only predicted the rapid advancement of technology but also underscored the importance of continuous research and development.

$$N(t) = N_0 \times 2^{\frac{t}{T}} \tag{18}$$

Here, $N(t)$ represents the number of transistors at time t, N_0 is the initial number of transistors, and T is the time period (typically two years) for the doubling effect. This equation encapsulates Moore's vision of growth in the semiconductor industry, a vision heavily influenced by the pioneering work done at Bell Labs.

Conclusion: The Enduring Impact of Bell Labs on Moore's Legacy

The role of Bell Labs' researchers in shaping Gordon Moore's career cannot be overstated. Their groundbreaking work laid the foundation for the semiconductor industry and provided Moore with the intellectual tools necessary to innovate. The collaborative and experimental culture of Bell Labs inspired Moore to pursue excellence in technology and leadership, ultimately leading to the establishment of Intel and the microprocessor revolution.

In summary, the researchers at Bell Labs were not just contemporaries of Moore; they were catalysts for his intellectual growth and professional development. Their influence is evident in Moore's contributions to the technology sector, his management philosophy, and his enduring legacy in the world of computing. As we reflect on Moore's journey, it is clear that the spirit of innovation fostered at Bell Labs continues to resonate in the technological advancements of today.

The Nobel Prize and Its Influence on Moore's Path

The Nobel Prize, often regarded as the pinnacle of achievement in various fields, holds a unique significance in the world of science and technology. For Gordon Moore, the co-founder of Intel and the architect of Moore's Law, the influence of the Nobel Prize transcended mere recognition; it shaped his career trajectory and the very fabric of the semiconductor industry.

The Nobel Prize in Physics: A Catalyst for Innovation

In 1956, the Nobel Prize in Physics was awarded to John Bardeen, Walter Brattain, and William Shockley for their groundbreaking work on the transistor at Bell Labs. This invention revolutionized electronics and laid the groundwork for modern computing. The transistor, a semiconductor device used to amplify or switch electronic signals, became the cornerstone of all subsequent advancements in technology.

Moore, who was deeply influenced by the developments at Bell Labs, recognized the potential of the transistor beyond its immediate applications. He understood that the evolution of this technology would lead to a paradigm shift in the way information was processed and stored. The recognition of the inventors by the Nobel Committee not only validated their work but also highlighted the importance of innovation in the semiconductor field.

Moore's Law: A Vision Inspired by Recognition

The concept that would later be known as Moore's Law—an observation that the number of transistors on a microchip doubles approximately every two years—was born from this fertile ground of innovation and recognition. The Nobel Prize served as a beacon, illuminating the path for aspiring engineers and scientists, including Moore. It instilled a sense of urgency and ambition within him to push the boundaries of what was possible in semiconductor technology.

Mathematically, Moore's Law can be expressed as:

$$N(t) = N_0 \cdot 2^{\frac{t}{T}}$$

where: - $N(t)$ is the number of transistors at time t, - N_0 is the initial number of transistors, - T is the doubling time (approximately 2 years).

This equation encapsulates the exponential growth that Moore envisioned for semiconductor technology, driven by the innovations recognized by the Nobel Prize.

The Ripple Effect of the Nobel Prize on Moore's Career

The impact of the Nobel Prize on Moore's career was multifaceted. Firstly, it motivated him to pursue his research with a fervor that would later define his leadership at Intel. The recognition of the significance of semiconductor technology by the Nobel Committee encouraged Moore to view his work not just as a job but as a contribution to a larger narrative of technological progress.

Moreover, the prestige associated with the Nobel Prize attracted top talent to the field, creating a competitive environment that spurred innovation. Moore capitalized on this by fostering a culture of creativity and experimentation at Intel. He understood that the key to sustaining growth in the semiconductor industry lay in attracting brilliant minds and encouraging them to think outside the box.

Challenges and Ethical Considerations

While the Nobel Prize inspired many, it also brought challenges. The pressure to innovate and outperform competitors was immense. Moore faced ethical dilemmas regarding the environmental impact of semiconductor manufacturing and the implications of rapid technological advancement on society. The recognition of the importance of his work came with the responsibility to ensure that progress did not come at the cost of ethical considerations.

Moore's commitment to addressing these challenges was evident in the establishment of the Gordon and Betty Moore Foundation, which aimed to support environmental conservation and scientific research. This philanthropic endeavor was a direct response to the recognition and success he achieved in his career, demonstrating that the influence of the Nobel Prize extended beyond personal accolades to a broader commitment to societal well-being.

Conclusion: The Lasting Legacy of the Nobel Prize on Moore's Path

In summary, the Nobel Prize played a pivotal role in shaping Gordon Moore's career and the semiconductor industry. It served as a catalyst for innovation, inspiring a generation of engineers and scientists to push the boundaries of technology. Moore's Law, a testament to his vision, continues to guide the trajectory of computing, while the ethical considerations that arose from this recognition highlight the responsibilities that accompany technological advancement.

As we reflect on the influence of the Nobel Prize on Moore's path, it is clear that recognition in science and technology can inspire not only individual achievement but also collective progress, shaping the future of industries and society as a whole.

The Birth of Intel: From Garage to Global Domination

Noyce and Moore: A Partnership Forged

The Meeting of Minds

In the annals of technological history, few partnerships have been as transformative as that of Gordon Moore and Robert Noyce. Their meeting was not merely a convergence of two brilliant minds; it was the ignition of a revolution that would reshape the very fabric of modern computing. To understand the significance of their collaboration, one must first appreciate the context in which it emerged.

The Early Days

In the early 1960s, the semiconductor industry was still in its infancy. The transition from vacuum tubes to transistors had opened new avenues for electronic innovation, yet the potential of silicon-based technology was largely untapped. Moore, with his keen analytical mind and a background steeped in chemistry and physics, was already making waves at Fairchild Semiconductor. Noyce, on the other hand, was not just a brilliant physicist; he was a visionary who had co-invented the integrated circuit. Their paths crossed in a landscape ripe for disruption.

The Catalyst for Change

Their initial meeting was serendipitous, born out of a shared vision for the future of electronics. At Fairchild, Moore was deeply involved in the development of silicon transistors, while Noyce was captivated by the idea of integrating multiple functions onto a single chip. The two men quickly recognized that their complementary skills could lead to groundbreaking advancements.

41

$$\text{Innovation} = f(\text{Collaboration, Vision, Execution}) \qquad (19)$$

This equation encapsulates the essence of their partnership. Their collaboration was fueled by a shared vision: to harness the power of silicon to create a new generation of computing devices. The execution of this vision would require not only technical prowess but also a willingness to challenge the status quo.

Founding Intel

In 1968, buoyed by their ambitions and the desire to break free from the constraints of Fairchild, Moore and Noyce, along with a handful of other engineers, founded Intel Corporation. The name "Intel" was derived from "Integrated Electronics," a nod to their commitment to pioneering the integrated circuit technology that would soon revolutionize the computing landscape.

As they embarked on this new venture, they faced a myriad of challenges. The semiconductor market was competitive and fraught with uncertainty, yet their determination to innovate propelled them forward. Noyce's charisma and leadership complemented Moore's analytical rigor, creating a dynamic synergy that would become the hallmark of Intel's culture.

The First Major Breakthrough

Intel's first significant product, the 3101 Schottky bipolar RAM, was a modest success, but it was the launch of the Intel 4004 microprocessor in 1971 that marked a watershed moment in the industry. The 4004 was the world's first commercially available microprocessor, a feat that was made possible by the duo's relentless pursuit of miniaturization and efficiency.

$$\text{Processing Power} \propto \frac{1}{\text{Transistor Size}} \qquad (20)$$

This relationship, which illustrates how processing power increases as transistor size decreases, was central to Moore's Law—an observation made by Moore himself in 1965 that the number of transistors on a chip would double approximately every two years. This principle not only guided Intel's design philosophy but also served as a roadmap for the entire semiconductor industry.

The Dynamic Duo in Action

The partnership between Moore and Noyce was characterized by mutual respect and a shared commitment to innovation. They complemented each other in ways that transcended mere technical collaboration. Moore's analytical mindset allowed him to foresee trends and opportunities, while Noyce's visionary leadership inspired their team to push boundaries. Together, they cultivated an environment where creativity thrived, and experimentation was encouraged.

Their meetings were often a blend of spirited discussions and intense brainstorming sessions. They debated the potential of new technologies, shared insights from their respective fields, and challenged each other's assumptions. This intellectual camaraderie was pivotal in shaping Intel's strategic direction.

The Importance of Complementary Skills

The success of Moore and Noyce's collaboration can largely be attributed to their complementary skills. Moore's scientific background provided a strong foundation for technological innovation, while Noyce's entrepreneurial spirit fueled the company's growth. Their ability to balance each other's strengths and weaknesses created a robust framework for decision-making.

For instance, when faced with the decision to pivot from memory chips to microprocessors, it was their combined expertise that led to the successful launch of the 4004. Moore's technical insights identified the feasibility of the design, while Noyce's market acumen recognized the growing demand for computing power in consumer products.

Conclusion

The meeting of minds between Gordon Moore and Robert Noyce was not just a historical footnote; it was the catalyst for a technological revolution that continues to resonate today. Their partnership laid the groundwork for Intel's rise to prominence and set the stage for the microprocessor era. As they forged ahead, they not only transformed their company but also redefined the possibilities of technology, proving that when brilliant minds unite, the results can be nothing short of extraordinary.

From Fairchild to Intel

The journey from Fairchild Semiconductor to the founding of Intel is a tale woven with ambition, innovation, and a touch of serendipity. In the early 1960s, Fairchild Semiconductor was at the forefront of the semiconductor revolution, having pioneered the production of silicon transistors and integrated circuits. The company's founders, including Robert Noyce and Gordon Moore, were instrumental in shaping the landscape of modern electronics. However, as the semiconductor industry began to evolve, so too did the aspirations of its key players.

The Seeds of Innovation

At Fairchild, Noyce and Moore worked alongside a cadre of brilliant engineers who would later become legends in their own right. The environment at Fairchild was one of intense creativity and competition, fostering an atmosphere where groundbreaking ideas could flourish. However, despite the company's success, the founders felt constrained by corporate bureaucracy and the limitations of existing technology.

The pivotal moment came when Noyce and Moore recognized the potential of microprocessors. They envisioned a future where computing power could be condensed into a single chip, revolutionizing the way technology would be used in everyday life. This vision was not without its challenges, as the complexity of designing and fabricating such chips was daunting. Nonetheless, the pair believed that with the right team and resources, they could make this vision a reality.

The Breakaway

In 1968, after a series of strategic discussions and reflections on their career trajectories, Noyce and Moore made the bold decision to leave Fairchild. They were not alone in this endeavor; a group of like-minded engineers, including the talented Andy Grove, joined them in this new venture. This exodus from Fairchild was driven by a desire for greater creative freedom and the opportunity to explore uncharted territories in semiconductor technology.

The new company, named Intel (short for Integrated Electronics), was founded in July 1968 in Mountain View, California. From the outset, Intel was positioned to be a leader in the burgeoning field of microelectronics. The founders were determined to create a culture that prioritized innovation, speed, and responsiveness to market needs—principles that would define Intel's trajectory for decades to come.

Establishing a New Paradigm

Intel's first product, the 3101 Schottky TTL RAM, was a modest beginning, but it laid the groundwork for the company's future innovations. However, it was the development of the microprocessor that would catapult Intel into the spotlight. In 1971, Intel introduced the 4004, the world's first commercially available microprocessor, which contained approximately 2,300 transistors and could perform up to 60,000 operations per second.

The significance of the 4004 cannot be overstated. It represented a paradigm shift in computing, as it allowed for the integration of processing power onto a single chip. This innovation not only paved the way for personal computers but also transformed industries ranging from telecommunications to consumer electronics. The success of the 4004 set the stage for subsequent microprocessors, including the 8008 and 8080, which further solidified Intel's reputation as a leader in the semiconductor industry.

Challenges and Triumphs

While the transition from Fairchild to Intel was marked by significant achievements, it was not without challenges. The early years of Intel were fraught with financial uncertainties and fierce competition. The founders had to navigate the complexities of raising capital, establishing a robust supply chain, and building a brand in a rapidly evolving market.

Despite these hurdles, Noyce, Moore, and their team demonstrated remarkable resilience and ingenuity. They leveraged their experience at Fairchild to streamline production processes and innovate in design, allowing Intel to stay ahead of competitors. The company's commitment to research and development ensured that it remained at the cutting edge of technology, continually pushing the boundaries of what was possible.

Conclusion

The transition from Fairchild Semiconductor to Intel was a defining moment in the history of computing. It marked the beginning of a new era characterized by rapid technological advancement and the democratization of computing power. Gordon Moore and Robert Noyce's vision, coupled with their unwavering determination, laid the foundation for what would become one of the most influential companies in the world.

As Intel grew, it not only transformed the semiconductor industry but also set the stage for the digital revolution that would follow. The legacy of this transition continues to resonate today, as the principles of innovation and collaboration established by Moore and his peers remain integral to the tech industry.

$$\text{Performance} \propto \frac{\text{Transistor Count}}{\text{Chip Area}} \tag{21}$$

This equation encapsulates the essence of Moore's Law, which states that the number of transistors on a microchip doubles approximately every two years, leading to an exponential increase in performance while simultaneously reducing costs. This principle guided Intel's development strategy and was instrumental in its rise to dominance in the semiconductor landscape.

In summary, the journey from Fairchild to Intel was not merely a transition between companies; it was a leap into the future of technology, driven by the vision and tenacity of its founders. As we delve deeper into the microprocessor revolution, we will explore how Moore's foresight and leadership shaped Intel's trajectory and impacted the world at large.

The Dynamic Duo in Action

In the annals of technology history, few partnerships have proven as pivotal as that of Gordon Moore and Robert Noyce. Their collaboration at Intel not only reshaped the semiconductor industry but also laid the groundwork for the digital age. This section delves into the synergy of their talents, the challenges they faced, and the remarkable innovations that emerged from their alliance.

Complementary Skills

Moore and Noyce's partnership was characterized by a unique blend of complementary skills. Moore, with his analytical prowess and deep understanding of semiconductor physics, approached problems with a meticulous, data-driven mindset. Noyce, on the other hand, was a visionary with an innate ability to inspire and lead. His charisma and entrepreneurial spirit were crucial in navigating the chaotic landscape of a burgeoning tech industry.

The combination of Moore's technical expertise and Noyce's leadership resulted in a formidable force. For instance, when faced with the challenge of creating a new microprocessor, Moore's insights into materials and fabrication processes allowed the team to innovate, while Noyce's strategic vision helped to secure funding and market positioning.

The First Major Breakthrough: The Intel 4004

The collaboration bore fruit with the launch of the Intel 4004, the world's first commercially available microprocessor, in 1971. The development of the 4004 was not without its challenges. The team had to overcome significant technical hurdles, including miniaturizing components and optimizing circuit designs.

The design process involved complex equations governing the behavior of transistors, such as the current-voltage relationship described by the Shockley equation:

$$I_D = I_S \left(e^{\frac{V_{GS}}{V_T}} - 1 \right) \tag{22}$$

where I_D is the drain current, I_S is the saturation current, V_{GS} is the gate-source voltage, and V_T is the threshold voltage. This equation encapsulated the fundamental principles that Moore and his team had to manipulate to achieve the desired performance.

The Intel 4004 revolutionized computing by integrating thousands of transistors onto a single chip, making it possible to create more compact and efficient systems. This breakthrough was not just a technical achievement; it also marked the beginning of the microprocessor era, fundamentally altering how computers were designed and used.

Scaling Up: The Intel 8008 and 8080

Building on the success of the 4004, Moore and Noyce pushed the boundaries further with the introduction of the Intel 8008 and 8080 microprocessors. These chips expanded the capabilities of personal computing and introduced new programming possibilities.

The Intel 8008, launched in 1972, was the first 8-bit microprocessor and allowed for more complex computations. The architecture of the 8008 can be described using the following equation for its instruction cycle:

$$T = T_{fetch} + T_{execute} \tag{23}$$

where T is the total time for an instruction cycle, T_{fetch} is the time taken to fetch the instruction from memory, and $T_{execute}$ is the time taken to execute the instruction. This simple model helped engineers optimize performance and understand the limitations of their designs.

The subsequent release of the Intel 8080 in 1974 further solidified Intel's position in the market. It was the first microprocessor to support a full set of instructions, enabling the development of more sophisticated software applications. The success of these processors was a testament to the dynamic collaboration between Moore and Noyce, showcasing their ability to innovate under pressure.

The Dawn of Personal Computing

The innovations brought forth by Moore and Noyce were instrumental in the rise of personal computing. Their vision for accessible technology transformed computers from room-sized behemoths into devices that could fit on a desk. This democratization of technology is encapsulated in Moore's Law, which posits that the number of transistors on a microchip doubles approximately every two years, leading to exponential increases in computing power.

The impact of this philosophy was profound. As Moore famously stated, "The number of transistors on a chip will continue to double approximately every two years. This is not a prediction, it's an observation." This observation became a guiding principle for the industry, driving relentless innovation and competition.

Fostering a Culture of Innovation

Moore and Noyce understood that technological advancements were not solely the result of individual brilliance but also of a supportive and dynamic corporate culture. They cultivated an environment at Intel that encouraged creativity, risk-taking, and collaboration. This culture was reflected in the company's open communication policies and its willingness to invest in research and development.

An example of this culture in action was the establishment of Intel's "15% rule," which allowed engineers to dedicate a portion of their time to projects of their choosing. This initiative led to groundbreaking innovations and a sense of ownership among employees, fostering loyalty and commitment to the company's mission.

Conclusion

The dynamic duo of Gordon Moore and Robert Noyce exemplifies how complementary skills and shared vision can lead to revolutionary advancements. Their partnership not only birthed the microprocessor but also set the stage for the digital revolution that followed. Through their collaboration, they transformed the landscape of technology and left an indelible mark on the world, proving that great minds truly think alike.

As we reflect on their contributions, it becomes clear that the legacy of Moore and Noyce extends beyond their technical achievements; it is a testament to the power of collaboration and innovation in shaping the future.

The Importance of Complementary Skills

In the world of technology and innovation, the synergy between individuals with complementary skills can lead to groundbreaking advancements. This principle is vividly illustrated in the partnership of Gordon Moore and Robert Noyce, co-founders of Intel. Their collaboration exemplifies how diverse talents can converge to create a powerhouse of innovation that reshapes entire industries.

Defining Complementary Skills

Complementary skills refer to the diverse abilities and expertise that, when combined, enhance the effectiveness and creativity of a team. In the context of Moore and Noyce, their distinct backgrounds and strengths allowed them to tackle challenges from multiple perspectives. Moore, with his deep understanding of semiconductor physics and analytical prowess, complemented Noyce's visionary leadership and engineering ingenuity. This dynamic interplay was crucial in navigating the complexities of the rapidly evolving tech landscape.

Theoretical Framework: Team Dynamics

Research in organizational behavior suggests that teams with complementary skills often outperform homogeneous groups. According to Belbin's Team Roles theory, individuals can be categorized into various roles based on their strengths, such as coordinators, implementers, and plant thinkers. Moore and Noyce represented a blend of these roles, allowing them to approach problems holistically.

For example, when faced with the challenge of developing the first microprocessor, their combined expertise facilitated innovative solutions. Moore's analytical thinking enabled rigorous evaluation of designs, while Noyce's creativity drove the vision for practical applications. This collaboration was not merely additive; it was multiplicative, leading to outcomes that neither could have achieved alone.

Practical Examples in Intel's Development

The importance of complementary skills is further illustrated in several key projects during Intel's formative years. One notable instance was the development of the Intel 4004, the world's first microprocessor. This project required not only technical expertise in chip design but also strategic foresight to identify market needs.

Moore's meticulous approach to engineering and Noyce's market insight were instrumental in shaping the product. Together, they navigated the technical hurdles of miniaturization and power efficiency while ensuring that the 4004 met the demands of emerging personal computing markets. This dual focus on technical excellence and market viability set Intel apart from its competitors.

The Role of Diversity in Problem-Solving

Diversity in skill sets fosters innovative problem-solving. Research indicates that teams with diverse expertise are better equipped to generate creative solutions. For instance, a study by Page (2007) in *The Difference: How the Power of Diversity Creates Better Groups, Firms, Schools, and Societies* posits that diverse teams outperform homogeneous teams in complex problem-solving scenarios.

In the case of Intel, the diversity of thought brought by Moore and Noyce allowed for rigorous debate and idea generation. They created an environment where challenges were met with a multitude of perspectives, ultimately leading to more robust solutions. This was particularly evident in their approach to scaling production and refining the manufacturing processes, where Noyce's operational insights complemented Moore's technical acumen.

Challenges of Complementary Skills

While complementary skills can lead to extraordinary outcomes, they also present challenges. Differences in approach and thought processes can lead to conflicts. For Moore and Noyce, navigating these differences required mutual respect and open communication.

One notable challenge arose during the transition from early product development to full-scale manufacturing. Noyce's emphasis on rapid market entry sometimes clashed with Moore's desire for perfection in engineering. However, their ability to reconcile these differences through constructive dialogue ultimately strengthened their partnership and led to better decision-making.

Conclusion: The Legacy of Complementary Skills

The partnership of Gordon Moore and Robert Noyce serves as a testament to the power of complementary skills in driving innovation. Their collaboration not only birthed Intel but also set the stage for the microprocessor revolution that transformed technology.

As the tech industry continues to evolve, the lessons learned from their partnership remain relevant. Emphasizing the importance of diverse skill sets within teams can lead to enhanced creativity, improved problem-solving, and ultimately, groundbreaking innovations. In a world where technology is advancing at an unprecedented pace, fostering complementary skills may be the key to unlocking the next wave of transformative ideas.

$$Innovation = Diversity + Collaboration \qquad (24)$$

In summary, the interplay of complementary skills not only defines successful partnerships but also shapes the future of technology, echoing the legacy of pioneers like Moore and Noyce.

The Road to the Microprocessor Revolution

The Revolutionary Intel 4004

In the annals of computing history, few inventions have had as profound an impact as the Intel 4004 microprocessor. Launched in 1971, this pioneering chip was not merely a product of its time; it was a harbinger of the personal computing revolution that would follow. The Intel 4004 was the first commercially available microprocessor, and its development marked a significant milestone in the evolution of technology, enabling a new era of computing that would forever change how we interact with machines.

The Birth of a New Era

The Intel 4004 was born out of a need for more compact and efficient computing solutions. Before its introduction, computers were large, cumbersome machines that occupied entire rooms. The idea of integrating the entire central processing unit (CPU) onto a single chip was revolutionary. The 4004 was designed by a small team at Intel, including engineers Federico Faggin, Ted Hoff, and Stan Mazor, who sought to create a microprocessor that would simplify the design of computers and make them more accessible to businesses and consumers alike.

Architecture and Specifications

The Intel 4004 was a 4-bit microprocessor, which means it could process 4 bits of data at a time. It featured a clock speed of 740 kHz and could execute approximately 92,000 instructions per second. The architecture of the 4004 was based on a simple yet effective design that included:

+ **Registers:** The 4004 had a set of 16 registers, each 4 bits wide, which allowed for efficient data manipulation.

+ **Instruction Set:** The microprocessor supported 46 different instructions, enabling it to perform arithmetic operations, data transfer, and control tasks.

+ **Memory Addressing:** It could address up to 64 KB of memory, a significant leap forward at the time.

The architecture of the 4004 is illustrated in Figure ??, showcasing its key components, including the ALU (Arithmetic Logic Unit), control unit, and data bus.

The Impact of the Intel 4004

The introduction of the Intel 4004 microprocessor had far-reaching implications for the computing industry. It laid the groundwork for the development of more advanced microprocessors and opened the door to personal computing. With its compact design and affordability, the 4004 enabled the creation of smaller, more efficient computers that could be used in a variety of applications, from business to education.

One of the most significant impacts of the 4004 was its role in the development of embedded systems. The microprocessor's ability to control devices and process data made it an ideal choice for applications in consumer electronics, automotive systems, and industrial machinery. The 4004's architecture paved the way for subsequent generations of microprocessors, including the Intel 8008 and 8080, which further expanded the capabilities of computing technology.

Real-World Applications

The Intel 4004 found its way into various applications shortly after its release. One of the most notable early uses was in calculators, where its processing power allowed for complex calculations to be performed quickly and efficiently. Additionally, the 4004 was utilized in the development of early personal computers, such as the Altair 8800, which became a catalyst for the home computing revolution.

Challenges and Limitations

Despite its groundbreaking nature, the Intel 4004 was not without its challenges. As a 4-bit processor, it had limitations in terms of data handling and performance compared to later 8-bit and 16-bit processors. This restricted its use in more demanding applications, leading to the rapid development of more powerful microprocessors. Furthermore, the design and manufacturing processes of the 4004 were complex and costly, which posed challenges for widespread adoption in the early years.

Conclusion: A Legacy of Innovation

The Intel 4004 microprocessor was a revolutionary product that changed the landscape of computing. Its introduction marked the beginning of a new era characterized by rapid technological advancements and the democratization of computing power. Gordon Moore's vision, encapsulated in the development of the 4004, set the stage for the exponential growth of the semiconductor industry and the emergence of personal computing as we know it today.

As we reflect on the legacy of the Intel 4004, it is essential to recognize its role as a catalyst for innovation. It not only transformed the way we think about computing but also inspired generations of engineers and technologists to push the boundaries of what is possible. The impact of the Intel 4004 continues to resonate in today's technology-driven world, reminding us of the power of vision, creativity, and collaboration in shaping the future.

Scaling Up: The Intel 8008 and 8080

The Intel 8008 and 8080 microprocessors marked pivotal moments in the evolution of computing, serving as critical stepping stones from early computing devices to the personal computers that would revolutionize the world. Developed in the early 1970s, these processors exemplified the rapid advancements in semiconductor technology and the growing demand for more powerful and efficient computing solutions.

The Intel 8008: A Leap Forward

Released in April 1972, the Intel 8008 was one of the first 8-bit microprocessors. It was designed to handle 8 bits of data simultaneously, allowing for more complex calculations and operations compared to its predecessors. The architecture of the 8008 was a significant departure from earlier models, introducing a more sophisticated instruction set that enabled programmers to develop more advanced applications.

Technical Specifications   The Intel 8008 featured:

+ **Data Bus Width:** 8 bits

+ **Address Bus Width:** 14 bits, allowing access to 16 KB of memory

+ **Clock Speed:** Initially up to 200 kHz

+ **Instruction Set:** 48 instructions, including arithmetic, logic, control, and data transfer operations.

The 8008's architecture included 7 registers, a program counter, a stack pointer, and a set of flags for conditional operations. This design enabled the processor to perform basic arithmetic operations, such as addition and subtraction, as well as more complex tasks involving data manipulation.

Challenges and Limitations

Despite its advancements, the Intel 8008 faced several challenges. The limited memory addressing capacity restricted its application in more demanding computing environments. Additionally, the complexity of programming for the 8008 was a barrier for many developers, as the instruction set required a deeper understanding of the hardware.

The Intel 8080: Building on Success

In 1974, Intel introduced the 8080 microprocessor, which built upon the foundation laid by the 8008. The 8080 was a more powerful and versatile chip that quickly became the backbone of early personal computing.

Technical Specifications   The Intel 8080 featured:

+ **Data Bus Width:** 8 bits

+ **Address Bus Width:** 16 bits, allowing access to 64 KB of memory

+ **Clock Speed:** Up to 2 MHz

+ **Instruction Set:** 78 instructions, including enhanced capabilities for arithmetic, logic, and control operations.

The 8080 also introduced additional registers and a more advanced interrupt system, which allowed for more efficient multitasking and improved responsiveness in applications. Its ability to interface with other components, such as memory and input/output devices, made it particularly appealing for developers.

Impact on Personal Computing

The introduction of the 8080 microprocessor was a game changer for the computing landscape. It provided the necessary processing power for the development of early personal computers, including the Altair 8800, which is often credited with sparking the personal computing revolution. The Altair 8800 utilized the 8080 processor and was one of the first computers to be sold as a kit, allowing hobbyists and enthusiasts to build their own machines.

Programming the 8080 Programming for the 8080 was facilitated by the availability of assembly language and higher-level languages like BASIC, which further democratized access to computing. The 8080's architecture supported various programming paradigms, enabling developers to create a wide range of applications, from simple games to complex business software.

Mathematical Foundations

The performance improvements of the 8008 and 8080 can be quantified through several mathematical concepts, including clock cycles and instruction throughput. The efficiency of a microprocessor can often be expressed in terms of MIPS (Million Instructions Per Second), which provides a measure of how many millions of instructions a processor can execute in one second.

For instance, if the 8080 could execute an average of 2,000 instructions in one second, its MIPS rating would be calculated as follows:

$$\text{MIPS} = \frac{\text{Number of Instructions Executed}}{\text{Execution Time in Seconds}} = \frac{2000}{1} = 2\,\text{MIPS}$$

This quantification illustrates the leap in processing power from the earlier 8008 to the 8080, which enabled developers to create more sophisticated software solutions.

Legacy and Conclusion

The Intel 8008 and 8080 microprocessors laid the groundwork for the microprocessor revolution, showcasing the potential of semiconductor technology to transform computing. Their influence is evident in the architecture of modern processors, and they remain a testament to the vision of Gordon Moore and his colleagues at Intel.

As the industry continued to evolve, the lessons learned from the development of the 8008 and 8080 informed future innovations, ultimately leading to the powerful and complex computing systems we rely on today. The legacy of these early microprocessors is not just in their technical specifications but also in their role in democratizing access to technology and paving the way for the personal computing era.

The Dawn of Personal Computing

The 1970s marked a pivotal moment in the history of computing, characterized by the emergence of personal computers (PCs) that would transform the way individuals interacted with technology. This era was fueled by advancements in microprocessor technology, particularly with Intel's groundbreaking 4004 and subsequent models that laid the foundation for personal computing.

The Intel 4004: A Revolution in Computing

The Intel 4004, introduced in 1971, was the world's first commercially available microprocessor. It represented a significant leap forward in computing technology, integrating the essential components of a computer's central processing unit (CPU) onto a single chip. This innovation drastically reduced the size and cost of computing devices, making them accessible to a broader audience. The architecture of the 4004 was based on a 4-bit word length and could address up to 640 bytes of memory, a remarkable feat for its time.

The significance of the 4004 can be encapsulated in the following equation, which illustrates the relationship between the number of transistors and the computational power of microprocessors:

$$\text{Computational Power} \propto \text{Transistor Count}^2 \qquad (25)$$

This equation reflects Moore's Law, which posited that the number of transistors on a chip would double approximately every two years, leading to exponential growth in computing power. The 4004's success set the stage for subsequent microprocessors, including the Intel 8008 and 8080, which further propelled the personal computing revolution.

The Rise of the Microprocessor: Intel 8008 and 8080

Following the 4004, the Intel 8008 was released in 1972, featuring an 8-bit architecture that allowed for greater data processing capabilities. This microprocessor could address 16 KB of memory and was instrumental in developing early personal computers. The 8008's architecture enabled more complex applications and laid the groundwork for the burgeoning software industry.

In 1974, Intel introduced the 8080, which became one of the most popular microprocessors of its time. The 8080's 8-bit architecture and ability to address up to 64 KB of memory made it a favorite among hobbyists and engineers. The 8080's success can be attributed to its versatility and the rise of a vibrant ecosystem of hardware and software developers who created innovative applications tailored to this new computing platform.

The Birth of the Personal Computer Market

As microprocessors became more powerful and affordable, the concept of personal computing began to take shape. In 1975, the Altair 8800, powered by the Intel 8080, was released and is often credited as the first commercially successful personal computer. This kit-based computer ignited the imagination of tech enthusiasts and hobbyists, leading to the establishment of a burgeoning market for personal computing.

The Altair 8800's success demonstrated that computers could be a tool for individuals, not just large corporations or research institutions. Its introduction inspired a wave of innovation, leading to the creation of software applications, operating systems, and user interfaces that would define the personal computing experience.

The Impact of Personal Computing on Society

The dawn of personal computing had profound implications for society. It democratized access to technology, allowing individuals to harness the power of computing in their homes and workplaces. This shift in technology usage fundamentally altered how people communicated, learned, and conducted business.

One of the most notable impacts was the rise of the software industry. Companies like Microsoft and Apple emerged, creating operating systems and applications that would become integral to the personal computing experience. The introduction of the Apple II in 1977, for example, showcased the potential of personal computers for education and entertainment, further solidifying the place of PCs in everyday life.

Challenges and Limitations

Despite the excitement surrounding personal computing, several challenges persisted. Early personal computers often faced limitations in processing power, memory, and user-friendliness. The complexity of programming and operating these machines posed a barrier to entry for many potential users.

Moreover, the lack of standardization in hardware and software created compatibility issues, complicating the user experience. These challenges necessitated the development of more intuitive interfaces and standardized protocols, paving the way for future advancements in personal computing.

Conclusion: A New Era of Computing

The dawn of personal computing, driven by the innovations of microprocessors like the Intel 4004, 8008, and 8080, marked a significant turning point in the technological landscape. This era not only democratized access to computing power but also laid the groundwork for the digital revolution that would follow. As individuals began to embrace personal computers, the stage was set for a future where technology would become an integral part of daily life, forever changing the way we interact with the world around us.

The legacy of this era continues to influence the development of technology today, as we explore new frontiers in computing that were once unimaginable. The journey from the first microprocessors to the sophisticated devices we use today exemplifies the relentless pursuit of innovation that defines the field of computing.

The Impact of Moore's Vision on the Microprocessor Industry

Gordon Moore's vision, encapsulated in what is now famously known as **Moore's Law**, has had a profound and lasting impact on the microprocessor industry. Originally articulated in 1965, Moore's Law posited that the number of transistors on a microchip would double approximately every two years, leading to an exponential increase in computing power while simultaneously decreasing relative cost. This prediction not only shaped the trajectory of semiconductor technology but also influenced the broader landscape of computing and technology at large.

The Exponential Growth of Transistor Density

The core of Moore's Law is the exponential growth in transistor density, which can be mathematically represented as:

$$N(t) = N_0 \times 2^{\frac{t}{T}} \tag{26}$$

where:

+ $N(t)$ is the number of transistors at time t,

+ N_0 is the initial number of transistors,

+ T is the doubling period (approximately 2 years).

This equation illustrates how the transistor count has increased over decades, leading to smaller, more powerful, and more energy-efficient processors. For instance, the Intel 4004, released in 1971, contained 2,300 transistors, while the Intel Core i9, released in 2017, boasts over 19 million transistors. This remarkable growth enabled the development of increasingly sophisticated applications, from personal computing to artificial intelligence.

Driving Innovation in Microprocessor Design

Moore's vision has also driven innovation in microprocessor design and architecture. As manufacturers sought to keep pace with the predicted growth, they explored new materials, manufacturing techniques, and architectural paradigms. The introduction of complementary metal-oxide-semiconductor (CMOS) technology allowed for the creation of smaller, faster, and more power-efficient chips. The transition from single-core to multi-core processors exemplifies how Moore's Law has spurred designers to maximize performance by increasing the number of processing units on a single die.

For example, the evolution from the Intel Pentium series to the Intel Core series illustrates this shift. The Pentium 4, released in 2000, featured a single-core architecture with a clock speed of up to 3.8 GHz. In contrast, modern Intel Core processors, such as the i7 and i9, utilize multiple cores, allowing for parallel processing and significantly improved performance in multi-threaded applications. This shift has been essential for meeting the demands of modern software, which increasingly relies on parallel processing capabilities.

Economic Implications and Market Dynamics

The impact of Moore's vision extends beyond technical advancements; it has significant economic implications as well. The reduction in cost per transistor has allowed for the democratization of technology, making powerful computing accessible to a broader audience. This phenomenon has fueled the growth of the consumer electronics market, driving demand for devices such as smartphones, tablets, and laptops.

As computing power became more affordable, it paved the way for the rise of the internet, cloud computing, and big data analytics. The ability to process vast amounts of data quickly has transformed industries ranging from finance to healthcare. Companies like Google and Amazon have leveraged this exponential growth to create services that rely on massive data processing capabilities, reshaping the way businesses operate.

Challenges and Limitations of Moore's Law

Despite its success, Moore's Law is not without its challenges. As transistors reach nanometer scales, physical limitations arise, including increased heat generation and quantum tunneling effects. These challenges have led to discussions about the potential end of Moore's Law, with some experts predicting that the traditional scaling of transistors may soon plateau.

For instance, the transition from 14 nm to 10 nm technology nodes has proven to be significantly more complex than previous generations, leading to delays in product launches and increased costs for manufacturers. The search for alternative materials, such as graphene and carbon nanotubes, is ongoing, as researchers explore ways to continue the trend of increasing transistor density.

Examples of Moore's Vision in Action

The impact of Moore's vision can be seen in numerous landmark products and innovations that have defined the microprocessor industry. For example, the launch of the Intel 8086 in 1978 marked the beginning of the x86 architecture, which remains the foundation for most personal computers today. This architecture has evolved over the years, with each new generation of processors building on the principles established by Moore's Law.

Another notable example is the smartphone revolution, where the integration of powerful microprocessors has transformed mobile computing. The Apple A-series chips, starting with the A4 in 2010, have demonstrated how Moore's vision can lead to the creation of highly efficient and powerful processors capable of handling complex tasks such as gaming, augmented reality, and machine learning.

Conclusion: The Enduring Legacy of Moore's Vision

In conclusion, Gordon Moore's vision has not only shaped the microprocessor industry but has also had far-reaching implications for technology and society as a whole. The exponential growth in transistor density, driven by Moore's Law, has enabled unprecedented advancements in computing power and has transformed the way we live and work. While challenges lie ahead, the legacy of Moore's vision continues to inspire innovation and creativity in the pursuit of new technological frontiers.

The journey from the early days of silicon transistors to the sophisticated microprocessors of today is a testament to the enduring impact of Gordon Moore's insights. As the industry navigates the complexities of modern technology, the principles laid out by Moore will undoubtedly guide future developments and innovations in the ever-evolving landscape of computing.

The Connection Between Moore's Law and Intel's Success

Gordon Moore's observation, famously known as Moore's Law, posits that the number of transistors on a microchip doubles approximately every two years, leading to an exponential increase in computing power while simultaneously reducing relative costs. This law, articulated in Moore's 1965 paper, not only served as a predictive guideline for the semiconductor industry but also became a cornerstone of Intel's strategic vision and operational practices. In this section, we will explore the profound connection between Moore's Law and Intel's meteoric rise to dominance in the technology sector.

Theoretical Underpinnings of Moore's Law

Moore's Law is not merely a statement about the doubling of transistors; it encapsulates a broader trend in technology, reflecting a continuous improvement in manufacturing processes, materials science, and design methodologies. The underlying theory can be expressed mathematically as:

$$N(t) = N_0 \cdot 2^{\frac{t}{T}} \tag{27}$$

where: - $N(t)$ is the number of transistors at time t, - N_0 is the initial number of transistors, - T is the time period over which the doubling occurs (approximately 2 years).

This exponential growth not only enhances performance but also drives down costs, leading to increased accessibility of computing technology. The implications of this growth are profound, as it enables a wider range of applications and innovations, ultimately shaping consumer behavior and industry standards.

Intel's Strategic Alignment with Moore's Law

Intel's strategic alignment with Moore's Law has been a pivotal factor in its success. The company has consistently invested in research and development (R&D) to push the boundaries of semiconductor technology. Intel's commitment to this law is evident in its annual roadmap, which outlines plans for new architectures and manufacturing techniques aimed at maintaining the pace of transistor scaling.

For instance, the introduction of the Intel 4004 in 1971 marked the first commercially available microprocessor, featuring 2,300 transistors. By 1974, the Intel 8080 had increased this number to 6,000, demonstrating a clear adherence to Moore's Law. This relentless pursuit of increasing transistor density allowed Intel to innovate rapidly and deliver products that outperformed competitors.

Challenges and Adaptations

Despite its successes, Intel has faced significant challenges in adhering to Moore's Law, particularly as physical limitations of silicon technology have emerged. As transistors approach atomic sizes, issues such as quantum tunneling and heat dissipation have become critical hurdles. These challenges necessitate innovative solutions, such as the development of new materials (e.g., graphene and silicon carbide) and advanced fabrication techniques like extreme ultraviolet (EUV) lithography.

One notable example of Intel's adaptation is the transition from planar transistors to FinFET (Fin Field-Effect Transistor) technology, which was introduced in the 22nm process node. This innovation allowed for greater control over transistor behavior, enabling further scaling while maintaining performance and power efficiency.

Impact on Market Dynamics

The connection between Moore's Law and Intel's success has also shaped market dynamics within the tech industry. As Intel consistently delivered products that adhered to the predictions of Moore's Law, it established itself as a leader in the microprocessor market, creating a competitive landscape where rivals were compelled to innovate rapidly to keep pace.

For example, AMD, Intel's primary competitor, has had to respond to Intel's advancements by developing its own high-performance processors. The competition has led to a cycle of innovation, where both companies push the envelope of what is possible in computing technology. The resulting arms race has benefited consumers through improved performance and lower prices.

Legacy and Continuing Relevance

As we look to the future, the relevance of Moore's Law remains a topic of debate. While some argue that the law is nearing its limits, others believe that new paradigms, such as quantum computing and neuromorphic chips, may extend the principles of exponential growth in computing power. Intel has actively engaged in these discussions, investing in next-generation technologies that could redefine the landscape of computing.

In conclusion, the connection between Moore's Law and Intel's success is a multifaceted relationship that encompasses theoretical, strategic, and market dynamics. By embracing the principles of Moore's Law, Intel has not only shaped its own destiny but has also played a critical role in the evolution of the entire technology sector. As we move forward, the challenge will be to sustain this momentum, ensuring that innovation continues to drive the industry into new frontiers of possibility.

Leadership and Innovation

Moore's Management Philosophy

Gordon Moore's management philosophy was a blend of innovation, collaboration, and a commitment to excellence, which significantly contributed to Intel's rise as a titan of the semiconductor industry. His approach was not merely about overseeing operations; it was about fostering a culture that prioritized creativity, accountability, and adaptability in an ever-evolving technological landscape.

Core Principles of Moore's Philosophy

At the heart of Moore's management style were several core principles that guided his decision-making and leadership:

- **Empowerment and Trust:** Moore believed in empowering his employees by trusting them to make decisions. He understood that innovation thrived in an environment where individuals felt valued and free to express their ideas. This empowerment was crucial in a fast-paced industry where rapid technological advancements were the norm.

+ **Collaboration over Hierarchy:** Rejecting rigid hierarchies, Moore promoted a collaborative work culture. He encouraged open communication across all levels of the organization, fostering an environment where ideas could flow freely, regardless of rank. This collaborative spirit was instrumental in the development of groundbreaking technologies at Intel.

+ **Focus on Innovation:** Moore's management philosophy placed a strong emphasis on innovation. He famously stated, "If you don't have a great idea, you're not going to be successful." This belief drove Intel to continually push the boundaries of what was possible, leading to the creation of revolutionary products like the microprocessor.

+ **Data-Driven Decision Making:** Moore advocated for a data-driven approach to management. He understood the importance of metrics and analytics in guiding business decisions. By relying on empirical data, Moore ensured that Intel's strategies were grounded in reality, allowing for more informed and effective decision-making.

+ **Long-Term Vision:** Moore had a knack for envisioning the future of technology. His foresight allowed him to make strategic decisions that positioned Intel for long-term success. This vision was encapsulated in what became known as **Moore's Law**, which predicted the exponential growth of computing power and guided the company's research and development efforts.

Application of Moore's Principles in Intel's Growth

Moore's management philosophy was not just theoretical; it was actively applied in Intel's operations, leading to significant milestones in the company's history. For instance, during the development of the Intel 4004, the world's first microprocessor, Moore's emphasis on collaboration and innovation was critical. Engineers from various departments worked together, sharing insights and expertise to overcome technical challenges. This collaborative effort resulted in a product that revolutionized computing.

Moreover, Moore's focus on data-driven decision-making was evident in Intel's approach to market analysis. By meticulously analyzing trends and consumer behavior, Intel was able to anticipate market needs and tailor its products accordingly. This adaptability was a key factor in the company's ability to dominate the microprocessor market.

Challenges and Criticisms

Despite the successes attributed to Moore's management philosophy, challenges and criticisms were inevitable. As Intel grew, maintaining the same level of empowerment and collaboration became increasingly difficult. The company faced issues related to bureaucracy and the complexities of managing a large organization. Critics argued that as Intel expanded, it risked losing the innovative spirit that had characterized its early years.

Additionally, the emphasis on data-driven decision-making sometimes led to analysis paralysis, where decision-makers became overly reliant on metrics and failed to act swiftly in a rapidly changing environment. Moore recognized these challenges and worked to adapt his management style, ensuring that Intel remained agile and responsive to market dynamics.

Legacy of Moore's Management Philosophy

The legacy of Gordon Moore's management philosophy is evident in Intel's enduring success and its influence on the tech industry as a whole. His principles of empowerment, collaboration, and innovation continue to resonate with leaders in technology and beyond. Companies seeking to replicate Intel's success often look to Moore's approach as a blueprint for fostering a culture of innovation.

In conclusion, Gordon Moore's management philosophy was a driving force behind Intel's transformation from a small startup to a global leader in technology. By prioritizing empowerment, collaboration, and a long-term vision, Moore created an environment where innovation could flourish, leaving an indelible mark on the semiconductor industry and inspiring future generations of leaders.

$$\text{Success} = \text{Innovation} \times \text{Collaboration} \times \text{Empowerment} \qquad (28)$$

Intel's Succession Plan: The Moore-Del Vecchio Era

The transition of leadership at Intel during the Moore-Del Vecchio era marked a significant chapter in the company's history, reflecting both the challenges and opportunities that arise when a pioneering founder steps aside. Gordon Moore, co-founder of Intel, had established a legacy of innovation and strategic foresight that would shape the semiconductor industry for decades. His partnership with Andy Grove, who served as CEO before transitioning to a more advisory role, set a high standard for leadership within the company. As Moore prepared to pass the torch, the importance of a well-defined succession plan became paramount.

The Importance of Succession Planning

Succession planning is a critical process in any organization, particularly in the fast-paced technology sector where change is the only constant. A successful succession plan ensures that a company can maintain its strategic direction and operational continuity in the face of leadership changes. In the case of Intel, Moore's foresight in establishing a robust succession plan was vital in mitigating the risks associated with leadership transitions.

Key Elements of the Moore-Del Vecchio Succession

The transition from Moore to Paul Otellini, and subsequently to Brian Krzanich, was characterized by several key elements:

+ **Leadership Development:** Moore and Grove emphasized the importance of cultivating leadership from within. This approach ensured that potential successors were not only familiar with Intel's culture but also had the necessary technical and managerial skills to lead effectively. This focus on internal talent development was crucial in maintaining Intel's competitive edge.

+ **Strategic Vision:** Moore's vision for Intel was not just about technology but also encompassed broader market trends and consumer needs. His strategic foresight helped shape the company's future direction, and this vision was communicated to potential successors to ensure alignment with Intel's long-term goals.

+ **Cultural Continuity:** The culture at Intel, often referred to as the "Intel Way," played a significant role in the company's success. Moore and his successors worked to instill this culture in new leaders, ensuring that the core values of innovation, risk-taking, and accountability remained intact.

+ **Mentorship:** Moore took an active role in mentoring his successors, sharing insights from his own experiences and emphasizing the importance of adaptability in a rapidly changing industry. This mentorship was instrumental in preparing leaders like Otellini and Krzanich for the challenges they would face.

Challenges Faced During the Transition

Despite the well-structured succession plan, the transition was not without its challenges. The semiconductor industry was experiencing rapid changes, including increased competition from emerging markets and technological shifts that demanded quick adaptation. The new leadership had to navigate these challenges while maintaining the legacy of innovation that Moore had established.

$$R = \frac{V}{I} \tag{29}$$

where R is resistance, V is voltage, and I is current. This equation symbolizes the challenges faced by Intel's leadership; as the voltage (or pressure to innovate) increased, so did the resistance (or challenges) that the new leaders had to overcome.

Examples of Leadership Decisions

Under the Moore-Del Vecchio leadership, several pivotal decisions highlighted the effectiveness of the succession plan:

+ **Investment in Research and Development:** Recognizing the rapid pace of technological advancement, Otellini and Krzanich prioritized R&D investments, which led to breakthroughs in microprocessor technology and solidified Intel's position in the market.

+ **Expansion into New Markets:** The leadership team made strategic moves to expand Intel's product offerings beyond traditional computing, venturing into mobile technology and data centers, aligning with Moore's original vision of a connected world.

+ **Focus on Sustainability:** The Moore Foundation's commitment to environmental sustainability influenced Intel's policies under Del Vecchio, leading to initiatives aimed at reducing the company's carbon footprint and promoting responsible manufacturing processes.

Conclusion: A Legacy of Leadership

The Moore-Del Vecchio era at Intel exemplifies the importance of a well-crafted succession plan in ensuring organizational resilience and continuity. By emphasizing leadership development, cultural continuity, and strategic foresight, Moore set the stage for future leaders to thrive. The challenges encountered during this transition only served to reinforce the need for adaptability and innovation, principles that remain at the heart of Intel's operations today.

In retrospect, the leadership transition not only preserved Moore's legacy but also positioned Intel to confront the complexities of a rapidly evolving technological landscape. As the company continues to navigate the future, the principles established during the Moore-Del Vecchio era will undoubtedly influence the next generation of leaders at Intel.

The Impact of Moore's Law

Gordon Moore's observation, famously articulated in 1965, that the number of transistors on a microchip doubles approximately every two years, has become a guiding principle in the semiconductor industry. This empirical law, which Moore later refined to predict exponential growth in computing power, has had profound implications for technology, economics, and society at large.

Understanding Moore's Law

Mathematically, Moore's Law can be expressed as:

$$N(t) = N_0 \cdot 2^{\frac{t}{T}} \tag{30}$$

where:

+ $N(t)$ is the number of transistors at time t,

+ N_0 is the initial number of transistors,

+ T is the doubling time (approximately 2 years),

+ t is the elapsed time in years.

This equation illustrates the exponential growth in transistor density, which in turn leads to increased performance and reduced cost per transistor. The implications of this growth are multifaceted, affecting everything from the design of consumer electronics to large-scale data processing and artificial intelligence.

Technological Advancements

The impact of Moore's Law is best exemplified through significant technological advancements over the decades. The introduction of the Intel 4004 in 1971 marked the first commercially available microprocessor, containing a mere 2,300 transistors. Fast forward to the Intel Core i9-11900K, which boasts over 19 million transistors. This staggering increase in transistor count has enabled the development of more powerful and efficient processors capable of handling complex computations and multitasking with ease.

Economic Implications

Moore's Law has also had profound economic implications. The consistent reduction in cost per transistor has led to the democratization of technology. As prices drop, more individuals and businesses gain access to powerful computing resources. This phenomenon has catalyzed the growth of the personal computer market in the 1980s, the rise of mobile computing in the 2000s, and the current expansion of cloud computing services.

The economic model built around Moore's Law has led to a cycle of innovation, where companies invest in research and development to stay ahead of competitors, resulting in a rapid pace of technological progress.

Challenges and Limitations

However, the relentless march of Moore's Law is not without its challenges. As transistors shrink towards atomic scales, engineers face significant physical limitations. Issues such as quantum tunneling, heat dissipation, and power consumption become increasingly problematic. The industry is now exploring alternative materials, such as graphene and carbon nanotubes, and new computing paradigms, such as quantum computing, to continue the trend of increased performance.

Cultural and Societal Impact

Beyond economics and technology, Moore's Law has influenced culture and society. The rapid advancement of computing technology has transformed industries, created new job markets, and reshaped daily life. The proliferation of smartphones, social media, and the Internet of Things (IoT) has altered how we communicate, work, and interact with the world around us.

The Future of Moore's Law

As we look to the future, the question arises: Is Moore's Law sustainable? While some experts predict that we may reach the physical limits of silicon-based technology, the spirit of Moore's Law continues to inspire innovation. New approaches, such as neuromorphic computing and advances in artificial intelligence, suggest that the quest for increased computational power will persist, albeit in forms that may diverge from traditional transistor scaling.

In conclusion, the impact of Moore's Law extends far beyond the confines of semiconductor physics. It has shaped the trajectory of technology, influenced economic models, and transformed society. As we navigate the challenges ahead, the legacy of Gordon Moore's vision will undoubtedly continue to inspire future generations of innovators and thinkers.

Conclusion

Moore's Law remains a testament to the power of foresight and the relentless pursuit of progress. As we stand on the brink of new technological frontiers, the principles underlying Moore's Law will guide us in our journey toward a future where computing capabilities continue to expand, driving innovation and enhancing the human experience.

Fostering a Culture of Innovation at Intel

In the high-octane world of technology, innovation is the lifeblood that drives success. At Intel, this was not merely a goal but a cultural cornerstone, meticulously nurtured under the leadership of Gordon Moore and his contemporaries. The ethos of innovation at Intel can be encapsulated through a multifaceted approach that intertwines organizational structure, employee empowerment, and a relentless pursuit of excellence.

The Innovation Framework

Intel's culture of innovation was anchored in its organizational framework. Moore believed that a flat organizational structure would facilitate open communication and collaboration. This structure encouraged employees to share ideas freely, breaking down silos that often stifle creativity. The concept of *cross-functional teams* became a hallmark of Intel's approach, allowing diverse perspectives to converge on complex problems. As a result, employees felt empowered to contribute, knowing their voices would be heard.

Employee Empowerment and Ownership

A pivotal aspect of fostering innovation was the emphasis on employee empowerment. Moore and his team implemented policies that encouraged risk-taking and experimentation. Employees were urged to think outside the box and were given the freedom to pursue projects that sparked their interest. This sense of ownership was critical; when individuals feel personally invested in their work, the quality of output improves significantly.

For instance, the development of the Intel 8086 microprocessor was a product of this empowering culture. Engineers were encouraged to explore unconventional designs, leading to a breakthrough that would set the stage for the personal computer revolution. The 8086 not only showcased Intel's technical prowess but also exemplified the innovative spirit that permeated the company.

Continuous Learning and Adaptation

To maintain its competitive edge, Intel adopted a philosophy of continuous learning. Moore understood that the tech landscape was ever-evolving, and staying ahead required a commitment to adaptation. This was formalized through initiatives such as *Intel University*, which provided employees with ongoing education in emerging technologies and market trends.

Furthermore, the concept of *fail fast, learn faster* became ingrained in Intel's culture. Employees were encouraged to view failures not as setbacks but as opportunities for growth. This mindset was crucial during the development of the Pentium microprocessor, where initial design flaws led to a rapid re-evaluation of processes and ultimately resulted in a more robust product.

Recognition and Reward Systems

Intel's culture of innovation was also reinforced through strategic recognition and reward systems. Moore understood that acknowledging employee contributions was vital for morale and motivation. Intel implemented various programs to celebrate innovative ideas, including the *Intel Achievement Award*, which recognized teams and individuals who made significant contributions to the company's success.

This recognition was not merely ceremonial; it was tied to tangible rewards, including bonuses and promotions. Such incentives encouraged employees to push boundaries and strive for excellence, knowing their efforts would be rewarded.

Collaboration with External Entities

In addition to internal initiatives, Intel actively sought collaboration with external entities, including universities, research institutions, and other tech companies. This approach allowed Intel to tap into a broader pool of ideas and innovations. Partnerships with academic institutions, for example, facilitated cutting-edge research that often translated into practical applications for Intel's products.

An exemplary case was Intel's collaboration with Stanford University on semiconductor research, which not only advanced technological understanding but also fostered a culture of innovation that extended beyond Intel's walls. This symbiotic relationship between academia and industry proved instrumental in maintaining Intel's leadership in semiconductor technology.

Conclusion

In conclusion, the culture of innovation at Intel was a carefully crafted ecosystem that thrived on employee empowerment, continuous learning, recognition, and external collaboration. Under Gordon Moore's leadership, Intel not only revolutionized the semiconductor industry but also set a standard for how a company could foster an environment where innovation flourished. This enduring legacy continues to inspire future generations of technologists and entrepreneurs, reminding us that the key to success lies in nurturing creativity and embracing change.

The Influence of Moore's Leadership on Intel's Employees

Gordon Moore's leadership at Intel was characterized by a unique blend of vision, innovation, and a deep commitment to fostering a culture that empowered employees. This section delves into the multifaceted influence Moore had on Intel's workforce, exploring how his management philosophy and strategic decisions shaped the company's environment and ultimately contributed to its success.

Empowerment through Innovation

Moore's approach to leadership was heavily influenced by his belief in the power of innovation. He understood that the semiconductor industry was not just about manufacturing chips; it was about creating a culture where creativity could flourish. Moore famously stated, "If you can't innovate, you can't lead." This mantra resonated throughout Intel and encouraged employees to think outside the box.

To facilitate innovation, Moore implemented several key initiatives. One of the most significant was the establishment of small, cross-functional teams that were tasked with developing new technologies. These teams operated with a high degree of autonomy, allowing employees to take ownership of their projects. This empowerment resulted in groundbreaking products like the Intel 4004 microprocessor, which revolutionized computing.

A Commitment to Education and Growth

Moore believed that continuous learning was essential for both personal and professional growth. He championed the idea that Intel should invest in its employees' education, providing them with opportunities to enhance their skills and knowledge. This commitment to education manifested in various forms, including:

- **In-House Training Programs:** Intel developed extensive training programs that covered a wide range of topics, from technical skills to leadership development. These programs were designed to keep employees at the forefront of technological advancements.

- **Sabbaticals and Advanced Degrees:** Moore encouraged employees to pursue further education by offering sabbaticals and financial support for advanced degrees. This not only enhanced employees' skills but also fostered loyalty and a sense of belonging within the company.

- **Mentorship Programs:** Recognizing the importance of mentorship, Moore established programs that paired experienced employees with newcomers. This initiative facilitated knowledge transfer and helped cultivate the next generation of leaders at Intel.

Fostering a Collaborative Environment

Another hallmark of Moore's leadership was his emphasis on collaboration. He understood that the best ideas often emerged from the collective efforts of diverse teams. To promote collaboration, Moore encouraged open communication and the sharing of ideas across all levels of the organization.

Moore's open-door policy allowed employees to approach him with their ideas and concerns, fostering a sense of trust and transparency. This accessibility not only made employees feel valued but also encouraged them to contribute actively to Intel's mission. As a result, many employees reported higher job satisfaction and a greater sense of purpose in their work.

Balancing Results and Employee Well-Being

While Moore was a results-driven leader, he also recognized the importance of employee well-being. He understood that a happy workforce was a productive workforce. To this end, he implemented policies that prioritized work-life balance, such as flexible work hours and generous vacation policies.

Moore's dedication to employee well-being was evident in his support for various health and wellness initiatives. Intel offered comprehensive health benefits, fitness programs, and mental health resources, ensuring that employees had access to the support they needed to thrive both personally and professionally.

The Legacy of Moore's Leadership

The influence of Gordon Moore's leadership on Intel's employees is perhaps best encapsulated in the company's enduring culture of innovation and excellence. His commitment to empowering employees, fostering collaboration, and prioritizing education has left an indelible mark on the organization.

As Intel continues to evolve in the rapidly changing tech landscape, Moore's legacy lives on in the values and practices that guide the company. Employees are still encouraged to think creatively, collaborate across disciplines, and pursue continuous learning. This culture not only attracts top talent but also positions Intel as a leader in the semiconductor industry.

In conclusion, Gordon Moore's leadership style profoundly shaped Intel's workforce, creating an environment where innovation thrived, and employees felt valued and empowered. His vision and commitment to fostering a collaborative and supportive culture have left a lasting impact that continues to inspire future generations of engineers and leaders in the technology sector.

The Challenges of Success: Industry Dominance and Ethical Dilemmas

The Intel Monopoly and Legal Battles

The U.S. vs. Intel: The Antitrust Story

The antitrust case against Intel Corporation is a pivotal chapter in the saga of Silicon Valley and the tech industry at large. In the late 1990s and early 2000s, Intel was not just a semiconductor giant; it was the dominant force in the microprocessor market, holding a staggering market share that often exceeded 80%. This dominance would soon attract the scrutiny of regulators and competitors alike, leading to a series of legal battles that would question the very fabric of competition in the tech industry.

Background of the Case

The roots of the antitrust case can be traced back to the competitive landscape of the semiconductor industry, which was characterized by rapid innovation and significant investments in research and development. Intel's microprocessors powered the majority of personal computers, making it a household name. However, with great power came great responsibility—or so the argument went.

In 1999, the Federal Trade Commission (FTC) began investigating Intel for potential antitrust violations. The crux of the allegations was that Intel had engaged in anti-competitive practices to maintain its monopoly. The FTC's concerns were centered around Intel's aggressive tactics against competitors, particularly Advanced Micro Devices (AMD), which had been trying to carve out a larger share of the market.

The Allegations

The FTC's investigation revealed several key allegations against Intel:

+ **Predatory Pricing:** Intel was accused of engaging in predatory pricing strategies to undercut competitors. This involved setting prices low enough to drive rivals out of the market, only to raise them once competition had been eliminated.

+ **Exclusive Contracts:** Intel allegedly entered into exclusive contracts with major computer manufacturers, such as Dell and HP. These contracts required manufacturers to use Intel processors exclusively, effectively locking AMD out of significant market opportunities.

+ **Deceptive Practices:** Intel was also accused of misleading marketing practices, where they allegedly misrepresented the performance capabilities of their processors compared to competitors.

Legal Proceedings

The legal proceedings began in earnest when the FTC filed a complaint against Intel in 2000. The case was emblematic of the broader concerns about monopolistic practices in the tech industry. Intel, in response, vehemently denied the allegations, arguing that its practices were competitive and aimed at innovation rather than exclusion.

The litigation process was lengthy and complex, involving numerous expert testimonies and extensive documentation. Intel's defense centered around the claim that its market dominance was a result of superior products and aggressive innovation rather than anti-competitive practices.

The Outcome

In 2009, after nearly a decade of legal wrangling, the FTC reached a settlement with Intel. While the settlement did not require Intel to admit wrongdoing, it mandated that the company change certain business practices. Intel agreed to refrain from engaging in exclusive contracts that would harm competition and to provide more transparency in its pricing strategies.

This outcome was significant as it set a precedent for how tech giants would be scrutinized in the future. The case underscored the importance of maintaining competitive markets, especially in industries characterized by rapid technological advancement.

Impact on the Industry

The antitrust case against Intel had far-reaching implications for the semiconductor industry and beyond. It served as a wake-up call for other tech companies, emphasizing the need for ethical business practices and transparency. Moreover, it highlighted the challenges of balancing innovation with competition—a delicate dance that continues to define the tech landscape.

The Intel case also paved the way for increased regulatory scrutiny of tech giants, a trend that has only intensified in recent years. As companies like Google, Facebook, and Amazon have risen to prominence, the lessons learned from the Intel antitrust case remain relevant.

In conclusion, the U.S. vs. Intel antitrust saga is a compelling narrative of power, competition, and the quest for fairness in the marketplace. It serves as a reminder that even the most innovative companies must navigate the complex waters of competition law to maintain their position in the industry.

$$\text{Market Share} = \frac{\text{Sales of Intel}}{\text{Total Sales in the Market}} \times 100\% \tag{31}$$

This equation illustrates how Intel's market share was calculated, reflecting the company's dominance in the microprocessor market during the late 20th century. The implications of the case continue to resonate, as the balance between innovation and competition remains a crucial aspect of the tech industry today.

The Fallout of the European Commission's Verdict

In 2009, the European Commission (EC) imposed a landmark fine of €1.06 billion on Intel Corporation for antitrust violations, marking a significant moment in the ongoing scrutiny of monopolistic practices in the tech industry. This verdict was not merely a legal decision; it was a clarion call for accountability in a rapidly evolving digital landscape. The EC found that Intel had engaged in practices that stifled competition and harmed consumers, particularly by offering substantial rebates to computer manufacturers on the condition that they exclusively used Intel chips. This section delves into the repercussions of the EC's ruling, exploring its implications for Intel, the semiconductor industry, and the broader context of antitrust regulation.

The Nature of the Violations

The European Commission's investigation revealed that Intel had employed a series of aggressive tactics aimed at maintaining its dominant market position in the microprocessor sector. Specifically, the Commission identified three primary anti-competitive practices:

+ **Exclusive Rebates:** Intel provided significant discounts to major PC manufacturers, such as Dell and HP, on the condition that they sourced all or most of their processors from Intel. This practice effectively locked competitors like AMD out of the market, as manufacturers were incentivized to favor Intel products to maximize their profit margins.

+ **Payments for Delays:** Intel was found to have paid manufacturers to delay the launch of products that featured rival processors. This tactic not only hindered competition but also delayed technological advancements that could benefit consumers.

+ **Predatory Pricing:** The EC accused Intel of engaging in predatory pricing strategies, where the company temporarily reduced prices on certain products below cost to undermine competitors' market positions and drive them out of the market.

These practices were viewed as clear violations of Article 102 of the Treaty on the Functioning of the European Union (TFEU), which prohibits the abuse of a dominant market position.

Immediate Consequences for Intel

The immediate fallout from the EC's verdict was multifaceted. Firstly, the substantial fine of €1.06 billion represented one of the largest penalties ever imposed by the European Commission in an antitrust case. This financial blow not only impacted Intel's bottom line but also served as a stark warning to other tech giants about the consequences of anti-competitive behavior.

Furthermore, the ruling forced Intel to reevaluate its business practices and marketing strategies. The company was compelled to alter its rebate structure and engage in more transparent dealings with manufacturers. This shift aimed to restore trust and foster a more competitive marketplace, while also mitigating the risk of further legal repercussions.

Broader Industry Implications

The EC's verdict against Intel had ripple effects throughout the semiconductor industry. Competitors such as AMD, who had long struggled against Intel's market dominance, saw a renewed opportunity to capture market share. The ruling emboldened smaller firms and startups, encouraging innovation and competition in a sector that had been heavily influenced by Intel's strategies.

Moreover, the case highlighted the need for stricter regulatory frameworks governing technology companies. The ruling prompted discussions among policymakers about the necessity of robust antitrust laws that could adapt to the unique challenges posed by the digital economy. As technology continues to evolve at an unprecedented pace, the lessons learned from Intel's case serve as a reminder of the importance of maintaining a competitive landscape that fosters innovation and protects consumer interests.

Long-term Effects on Antitrust Regulation

The fallout from the European Commission's verdict extended beyond Intel and the semiconductor industry. It reignited debates about the effectiveness of antitrust laws in the digital age. As tech giants like Google, Amazon, and Facebook have emerged as dominant players in their respective fields, the principles established in the Intel case have been invoked in subsequent investigations and regulatory actions.

Legal experts have pointed to the Intel case as a precedent that could shape future antitrust enforcement. The ruling underscored the importance of scrutinizing not only the actions of dominant firms but also the broader market dynamics that allow such behavior to flourish. The EC's willingness to impose significant penalties on powerful corporations signaled a shift towards a more aggressive stance on antitrust enforcement, encouraging regulators worldwide to take a closer look at the practices of major tech companies.

Conclusion

The European Commission's verdict against Intel was a watershed moment in the realm of antitrust regulation, with far-reaching implications for the tech industry and beyond. By holding Intel accountable for its anti-competitive practices, the EC not only safeguarded consumer interests but also set a precedent for future regulatory actions. As the digital landscape continues to evolve, the lessons learned from Intel's case will remain relevant, reminding us of the delicate balance between innovation and competition in an increasingly interconnected world.

Balancing Market Dominance and Fair Competition

The semiconductor industry, particularly through the lens of Intel's trajectory, has become a focal point for discussions surrounding market dominance and fair competition. As a pioneer in microprocessor technology, Intel's rise to prominence sparked debates about monopolistic practices and the ethical responsibilities of technology companies. This section delves into the challenges of maintaining a competitive landscape while navigating the complexities of market power.

Understanding Market Dominance

Market dominance occurs when a company holds a significant share of the market, allowing it to influence prices, production, and innovation. According to the *European Commission's Guidelines on the Assessment of Market Dominance*, a firm is considered dominant if it holds a market share of 40% or more, although this threshold can vary based on industry dynamics. In the case of Intel, its market share in the microprocessor sector often exceeded this threshold, leading to scrutiny from regulators and competitors alike.

$$\text{Market Share} = \frac{\text{Company Sales}}{\text{Total Market Sales}} \times 100\% \tag{32}$$

For instance, during the late 1990s and early 2000s, Intel's dominance was characterized by its overwhelming share of the x86 microprocessor market, which at one point reached nearly 90%. This level of control raised concerns about potential anti-competitive behavior, prompting investigations by various regulatory bodies.

The Role of Antitrust Laws

Antitrust laws are designed to promote fair competition and prevent monopolistic practices. In the United States, the Sherman Antitrust Act of 1890 serves as a foundational statute against anti-competitive conduct. Intel faced significant legal challenges under this framework, particularly when rival companies accused it of engaging in practices that stifled competition.

One notable case involved AMD (Advanced Micro Devices), which alleged that Intel used its market power to secure exclusive agreements with major PC manufacturers, effectively locking out competitors. The case highlighted the tension between fostering innovation and maintaining a level playing field in the marketplace.

$$\text{Profit Margin} = \frac{\text{Net Income}}{\text{Revenue}} \times 100\% \tag{33}$$

Intel's ability to maintain high profit margins—often exceeding 30%—was a double-edged sword. While it signaled operational efficiency and market leadership, it also drew the ire of regulators who viewed such margins as indicative of anti-competitive behavior.

Balancing Innovation with Competition

Balancing market dominance with fair competition is not merely a legal or ethical issue; it is also a matter of innovation. Companies like Intel invest heavily in research and development (R&D) to maintain their competitive edge. The challenge lies in ensuring that such investments do not translate into unfair advantages that stifle competition.

$$\text{R\&D Intensity} = \frac{\text{R\&D Expenditure}}{\text{Total Revenue}} \times 100\% \tag{34}$$

Intel's R&D intensity has historically been around 20%, a figure that underscores its commitment to innovation. However, this commitment must be matched by a willingness to foster an environment where competitors can also thrive. The introduction of new technologies, such as the Pentium and later the Core series, exemplified Intel's innovative prowess, yet these advancements also raised questions about whether they were achieved at the expense of fair competition.

Case Studies: Intel and Its Competitors

To illustrate the complexities of balancing market dominance with fair competition, we can examine two pivotal case studies: the legal battles with AMD and the emergence of ARM architecture as a competitive force in the mobile market.

The AMD Legal Battle   In 2005, AMD filed a complaint against Intel with the European Commission, alleging that Intel had engaged in anti-competitive practices by offering rebates to manufacturers for using Intel chips exclusively. This case not only highlighted the contentious nature of market dominance but also underscored the importance of regulatory oversight in maintaining competitive markets. The European Commission ultimately ruled against Intel, imposing a record fine of €1.06 billion in 2009.

The Rise of ARM   The emergence of ARM architecture as a formidable competitor in the mobile computing space further complicates the narrative of market dominance. ARM's business model, which licenses its technology to other manufacturers, contrasts sharply with Intel's traditional approach. This diversification of technology providers has led to increased competition, prompting Intel to adapt its strategies to remain relevant in a rapidly evolving market.

Ethical Considerations and Corporate Responsibility

As technology companies navigate the challenges of market dominance, ethical considerations become paramount. The responsibility of a dominant player extends beyond compliance with antitrust laws; it encompasses a commitment to fostering innovation while ensuring that competitors have the opportunity to succeed.

The establishment of the *Moore Foundation* by Gordon Moore serves as a testament to the belief in corporate responsibility. The foundation's focus on environmental stewardship and education reflects a broader understanding of the impact that technology companies can have on society.

Conclusion

In conclusion, balancing market dominance with fair competition presents a multifaceted challenge for technology companies like Intel. As they navigate legal frameworks, ethical considerations, and the imperative for innovation, the stakes are high. The lessons learned from Intel's journey underscore the importance of fostering a competitive landscape that not only drives technological advancement but also ensures a level playing field for all participants in the market.

As the industry continues to evolve, the dialogue surrounding market dominance and fair competition will remain critical. The future of computing depends on the ability of companies to innovate responsibly while respecting the principles of fair competition.

Ethical Conundrums: Balancing Innovation and Responsibility

The Moore Foundation: Philanthropy and Environmental Activism

Gordon Moore, renowned for his pivotal role in the semiconductor industry, extended his influence beyond the realm of technology through the establishment of the **Gordon and Betty Moore Foundation**. Founded in 2000, the foundation reflects Moore's commitment to philanthropy, focusing on environmental conservation, science, and patient care. This section delves into the foundation's initiatives and the ethical responsibilities that accompany such a legacy.

Foundation Overview

The Gordon and Betty Moore Foundation was established with a mission to foster scientific discovery, environmental conservation, and the promotion of patient care. With an endowment exceeding $5 billion, the foundation has funded numerous projects aimed at addressing some of the most pressing challenges facing our planet today.

Environmental Initiatives

One of the cornerstone initiatives of the Moore Foundation is its dedication to environmental stewardship. The foundation's **Environmental Conservation Program** focuses on protecting critical ecosystems, promoting sustainable practices, and combating climate change. A notable example of this commitment is the support for the *Marine Conservation Initiative*, which aims to protect marine biodiversity and promote sustainable fishing practices.

Key Projects

The foundation has funded various projects that illustrate its commitment to environmental activism:

- **The California Marine Protected Areas Initiative:** This project seeks to enhance the management of marine protected areas along the California coast. By supporting scientific research and community engagement, the initiative aims to ensure the resilience of marine ecosystems in the face of climate change.

- **The Amazon Rainforest Conservation Project:** Recognizing the Amazon's critical role in global biodiversity and climate regulation, the foundation has invested in efforts to protect large areas of this vital ecosystem. This includes partnerships with local organizations to promote sustainable land-use practices and combat deforestation.

- **The Global Climate Initiative:** In response to the urgent need for climate action, the foundation has supported initiatives aimed at reducing greenhouse gas emissions. This includes funding research on renewable energy technologies and advocating for policy changes that promote sustainability.

Philanthropy and Ethical Responsibility

The foundation's work raises important questions about the ethical responsibilities of philanthropists in the modern world. As technology companies like Intel grow in power and influence, the need for responsible stewardship of resources becomes paramount. Moore's philanthropic efforts exemplify a model for tech leaders to follow, emphasizing the importance of giving back to society.

Challenges and Controversies

Despite its noble mission, the Moore Foundation has faced challenges and controversies. Critics argue that large philanthropic organizations can exert undue influence on public policy and scientific research. For instance, the foundation's funding decisions may prioritize certain environmental issues over others, potentially sidelining critical areas that require attention. Additionally, the foundation has been scrutinized for its involvement in projects that may inadvertently support practices contrary to its stated mission.

A Legacy of Environmental Activism

The legacy of Gordon Moore is not solely defined by his contributions to technology but also by his commitment to philanthropy and environmental activism. The Moore Foundation serves as a testament to the potential for individuals in positions of power to effect positive change in society. Through its various initiatives, the foundation not only addresses immediate environmental concerns but also inspires future generations to consider the broader implications of their work.

In summary, the Gordon and Betty Moore Foundation exemplifies the intersection of technology, philanthropy, and environmental responsibility. As the world grapples with pressing challenges such as climate change and biodiversity loss, the foundation's initiatives highlight the importance of ethical stewardship and the role of philanthropy in fostering a sustainable future.

Conclusion

In conclusion, the Moore Foundation stands as a beacon of hope in the realm of environmental activism. Gordon Moore's vision extends beyond the semiconductor industry, embodying a commitment to philanthropy that prioritizes the health of our planet. As we navigate the complexities of the modern world, the foundation's work serves as a reminder of the profound impact that thoughtful, responsible action can have on future generations.

Controversies Surrounding Intel's Environmental Impact

The semiconductor industry, while a beacon of technological advancement, has not been without its environmental controversies. Intel, as one of the leading companies in this field, has faced scrutiny regarding its ecological footprint. This section explores the various controversies surrounding Intel's environmental impact, highlighting the challenges and criticisms the company has encountered over the years.

Chemical Waste and Pollution

One of the primary environmental concerns associated with semiconductor manufacturing is the generation of chemical waste. The production of microprocessors involves the use of various hazardous materials, including solvents, acids, and heavy metals. These substances pose significant risks to both the environment and human health if not managed properly.

In the early 2000s, Intel faced backlash for its practices regarding chemical waste disposal. Reports surfaced indicating that certain facilities were releasing toxic substances into the environment, leading to contamination of local water supplies. For instance, Intel's factory in Hillsboro, Oregon, was cited for improper disposal of hazardous waste, raising alarms among environmental groups and local residents. The company's response included pledging to improve waste management practices and invest in cleaner technologies.

Water Usage and Scarcity

Another critical issue is the substantial amount of water required for semiconductor manufacturing. The process consumes vast quantities of ultra-pure water for cooling and cleaning purposes. As water scarcity becomes an increasingly pressing global issue, companies like Intel have been challenged to balance their operational needs with sustainable water usage.

In 2019, Intel was criticized for its water consumption in Arizona, where the company was expanding its manufacturing facilities. Activists argued that the water used for semiconductor production could be better allocated to support local communities suffering from drought conditions. In response, Intel committed to implementing water conservation measures and aimed to achieve net positive water use by 2030, demonstrating a shift towards more sustainable practices.

Energy Consumption and Carbon Footprint

The energy-intensive nature of semiconductor manufacturing also raises environmental concerns. The production of microchips requires significant electrical power, contributing to the carbon footprint of the industry. As global awareness of climate change increases, Intel has faced pressure to reduce its energy consumption and transition to renewable energy sources.

Intel's manufacturing plants, referred to as "fabs," are often criticized for their high energy demands. According to a report by the International Energy Agency, semiconductor manufacturing accounted for approximately 1.5% of global electricity consumption in 2020. Critics have pointed out that without substantial changes, this figure could continue to rise, exacerbating climate change.

In response to these concerns, Intel has set ambitious sustainability goals. The company aims to achieve 100% renewable energy usage across its global operations by 2030. Additionally, Intel has invested in energy-efficient technologies and practices, such as advanced cooling systems and optimized manufacturing processes, to mitigate its environmental impact.

Community Relations and Environmental Justice

Intel's environmental practices have also raised questions about community relations and environmental justice. The proximity of semiconductor manufacturing facilities to residential areas has led to concerns about the health impacts of emissions and waste. Communities near Intel's factories have expressed fears about potential health risks, including respiratory issues and other long-term health effects associated with exposure to hazardous materials.

For example, in 2008, residents near Intel's facility in Santa Clara, California, reported health issues they believed were linked to emissions from the plant. This led to a series of community meetings and discussions about the company's environmental practices. In response, Intel launched community engagement initiatives aimed at addressing residents' concerns and fostering transparency about its operations.

Corporate Responsibility and Accountability

As a leader in the tech industry, Intel's commitment to environmental responsibility is under constant scrutiny. Stakeholders, including investors, customers, and advocacy groups, expect the company to take accountability for its environmental impact and demonstrate leadership in sustainability.

Intel has made strides in this area by publishing annual sustainability reports, outlining its environmental goals and progress. The company's commitment to transparency has been recognized, yet critics argue that more needs to be done. They urge Intel to adopt more stringent environmental standards and take proactive measures to address the controversies surrounding its operations.

Conclusion

The controversies surrounding Intel's environmental impact highlight the complex interplay between technological advancement and ecological responsibility. As the semiconductor industry continues to evolve, Intel's ability to navigate these challenges will be critical not only for its reputation but also for the broader implications for the environment. The company's ongoing efforts to mitigate its impact, engage with communities, and lead in sustainability will be pivotal in shaping the future of the tech industry and its relationship with the planet.

$$\text{Environmental Impact} = \frac{\text{Waste} + \text{Energy Consumption} + \text{Water Usage}}{\text{Sustainability Practices}} \quad (35)$$

This equation illustrates the balance that companies like Intel must achieve: minimizing environmental impact through effective sustainability practices while managing the inherent waste, energy consumption, and water usage associated with semiconductor manufacturing. The journey towards sustainable innovation is ongoing, and Intel's actions will serve as a barometer for the industry as a whole.

Addressing Labor Issues: Moore's Commitment to Workers' Rights

Gordon Moore's journey through the semiconductor industry was not only marked by technological innovations but also by a profound commitment to the welfare of workers. As Intel grew from a fledgling startup to a dominant force in the tech landscape, the complexities surrounding labor issues became increasingly significant. This section delves into Moore's dedication to addressing these challenges, the theoretical frameworks that informed his approach, and the practical implications of his policies.

Theoretical Frameworks: Labor Rights and Corporate Responsibility

At the heart of Moore's philosophy regarding labor issues was a belief in the fundamental rights of workers. This belief can be understood through the lens of several key theories:

+ **Social Contract Theory:** This theory posits that businesses owe a duty to their employees, akin to a social contract. Moore believed that as Intel prospered, it was essential to ensure that the benefits of this success were shared with the workforce. This perspective aligns with the notion that corporations are not merely economic entities but also social institutions with responsibilities to their employees.

+ **Stakeholder Theory:** Moore's commitment to workers can also be framed within stakeholder theory, which emphasizes that businesses should consider the interests of all stakeholders, including employees, customers, suppliers, and the community. By prioritizing workers' rights, Moore aimed to create a more equitable environment that fostered loyalty and innovation.

+ **Corporate Social Responsibility (CSR):** Moore's approach to labor issues was also informed by CSR principles, which advocate for businesses to operate ethically and contribute positively to society. Under his leadership, Intel implemented policies that not only addressed labor rights but also promoted employee well-being and community engagement.

Practical Steps Taken by Moore

Moore's commitment to labor rights manifested in several key initiatives and policies at Intel:

1. **Fair Labor Practices:** Moore was an advocate for fair labor practices, ensuring that Intel's operations adhered to ethical standards. This included promoting fair wages, reasonable working hours, and safe working conditions. Under his leadership, Intel adopted a code of conduct that emphasized respect for workers' rights and the importance of ethical labor practices.

2. **Employee Benefits and Support Programs:** Recognizing that a satisfied workforce is crucial for innovation and productivity, Moore championed comprehensive employee benefits. This included health insurance, retirement plans, and educational opportunities. By investing in employees' well-being, Moore aimed to create a loyal and motivated workforce.

3. **Open Communication Channels:** Moore believed in fostering an open dialogue between management and employees. He established communication channels that allowed workers to voice their concerns and suggestions. This not only empowered employees but also contributed to a culture of transparency and trust within the organization.

4. **Diversity and Inclusion Initiatives:** Understanding the importance of a diverse workforce, Moore implemented initiatives aimed at promoting diversity and inclusion within Intel. He recognized that a variety of perspectives could lead to greater innovation and problem-solving capabilities. This commitment to inclusivity extended to hiring practices and employee development programs.

Challenges and Controversies

Despite Moore's commitment to workers' rights, Intel faced its share of challenges and controversies regarding labor issues:

+ **Labor Relations and Unionization Efforts:** As Intel expanded, there were instances of labor unrest and calls for unionization. While Moore supported fair labor practices, the company's approach to unionization was often met with resistance. The complexities of managing labor relations in a rapidly evolving industry presented ongoing challenges.

+ **Global Labor Standards:** As Intel expanded its operations globally, ensuring consistent labor standards across different regions became increasingly difficult. Moore faced criticism regarding labor practices in countries where Intel operated, highlighting the challenges of maintaining ethical standards in diverse cultural contexts.

+ **Environmental and Labor Intersections:** The intersection of environmental issues and labor rights also presented challenges. Moore's commitment to environmental sustainability sometimes conflicted with labor practices, especially in regions where environmental regulations were lax. Balancing these interests required ongoing negotiation and adaptation.

Legacy of Moore's Commitment to Workers' Rights

Gordon Moore's dedication to addressing labor issues and promoting workers' rights left a lasting legacy within Intel and the broader tech industry. His commitment to ethical labor practices set a precedent for other companies, encouraging them to prioritize the welfare of their employees. The principles he championed continue to resonate in contemporary discussions about corporate responsibility and labor rights.

In conclusion, Moore's approach to labor issues was characterized by a deep understanding of the social and ethical responsibilities of corporations. By advocating for fair labor practices, comprehensive employee benefits, and open communication, he sought to create a workplace where innovation could thrive alongside a commitment to the well-being of workers. As the tech industry continues to evolve, Moore's legacy serves as a reminder of the importance of addressing labor issues in the pursuit of technological advancement.

The Ethical Responsibilities of Tech Companies in the Modern World

In the rapidly evolving landscape of technology, the ethical responsibilities of tech companies have become a pivotal concern. As the architects of innovations that shape our daily lives, companies like Intel, founded by visionaries such as Gordon Moore, must navigate a complex web of ethical dilemmas that arise from their influence on society. This section explores the multifaceted ethical responsibilities that tech companies face today, examining the implications of their decisions on individuals, communities, and the environment.

The Framework of Ethical Responsibility

At the core of ethical responsibility lies the principle of *corporate social responsibility* (CSR), which posits that businesses should not only focus on profit maximization but also consider the impact of their operations on society and the environment. According to [1], CSR encompasses four dimensions: economic, legal, ethical, and philanthropic responsibilities. For tech companies, these dimensions manifest in various ways:

- **Economic Responsibility:** Companies must ensure financial viability while creating value for stakeholders.

- **Legal Responsibility:** Compliance with laws and regulations governing technology and data usage is paramount.

- **Ethical Responsibility:** Beyond legal obligations, tech firms should adhere to ethical standards that promote fairness, transparency, and respect for user privacy.

+ **Philanthropic Responsibility:** Engaging in charitable activities and community support enhances a company's reputation and fosters goodwill.

Privacy and Data Protection

One of the most pressing ethical issues confronting tech companies is the management of user data. The advent of big data and artificial intelligence has enabled companies to collect, analyze, and leverage vast amounts of personal information. However, this capability raises significant ethical concerns regarding privacy and consent.

The General Data Protection Regulation (GDPR) implemented in the European Union serves as a benchmark for data protection, emphasizing the need for explicit consent and transparency in data handling. Companies must ensure that users are informed about how their data will be used and provide them with the option to opt-out. Failure to adhere to these principles can lead to severe reputational damage and legal repercussions, as seen in the case of Facebook's Cambridge Analytica scandal, where user data was misappropriated without consent, resulting in significant backlash and regulatory scrutiny.

Environmental Impact

Tech companies also face ethical responsibilities related to their environmental footprint. The production of electronic devices and data centers consumes substantial resources and generates e-waste, contributing to environmental degradation. According to the United Nations, electronic waste is one of the fastest-growing waste streams globally, with an estimated 50 million tons generated annually [2].

Companies like Intel have made strides in sustainability by implementing eco-friendly practices, such as reducing energy consumption in manufacturing processes and investing in recycling programs. However, the challenge remains to balance technological advancement with environmental stewardship. The ethical imperative is clear: tech companies must adopt sustainable practices that minimize their ecological impact and contribute to a circular economy.

Labor Practices and Human Rights

The global nature of the tech industry also brings forth ethical considerations regarding labor practices and human rights. Many tech companies rely on a complex supply chain that spans multiple countries, often including regions with lax labor regulations. Reports of poor working conditions, child labor, and exploitation in the production of electronic components have surfaced, raising ethical alarms.

For instance, the mining of rare earth minerals, essential for manufacturing electronic devices, has been linked to human rights abuses in countries like the Democratic Republic of Congo. Tech companies must ensure that their supply chains are ethical and transparent, adhering to principles outlined in frameworks such as the United Nations Guiding Principles on Business and Human Rights. This includes conducting due diligence to identify and mitigate risks associated with labor practices throughout the supply chain.

Algorithmic Bias and Fairness

As algorithms increasingly dictate decisions in areas such as hiring, lending, and law enforcement, the ethical implications of algorithmic bias have garnered attention. Algorithms are only as unbiased as the data they are trained on, and if that data reflects societal prejudices, the outcomes can perpetuate discrimination.

For example, a study by [3] revealed that a widely used algorithm for predicting recidivism in criminal justice disproportionately flagged Black defendants as high risk, despite similar rates of reoffending among different racial groups. Tech companies have a responsibility to ensure fairness and accountability in their algorithms, employing diverse teams to audit and refine their models to mitigate bias.

The Role of Stakeholders

Engaging with stakeholders is crucial for tech companies to address ethical responsibilities effectively. Stakeholders include employees, customers, investors, and the communities in which companies operate. By fostering open dialogue and soliciting feedback, tech companies can better understand the ethical implications of their actions and make informed decisions.

For instance, Intel has initiated programs to engage with stakeholders on sustainability issues, allowing them to voice concerns and contribute to the company's environmental strategy. This collaborative approach not only enhances transparency but also builds trust and accountability.

Conclusion

In conclusion, the ethical responsibilities of tech companies in the modern world are multifaceted and complex. From data privacy to environmental sustainability, labor practices, and algorithmic fairness, these companies must navigate a myriad of challenges that demand a commitment to ethical principles. As leaders in innovation, tech firms have the opportunity—and the obligation—to shape a future that prioritizes ethical considerations alongside technological advancement. Embracing these responsibilities not only benefits society but also enhances the long-term viability and reputation of the companies themselves.

Bibliography

[1] Carroll, A. B. (1991). The Pyramid of Corporate Social Responsibility: Toward the Moral Management of Organizational Stakeholders. *Business Horizons*, 34(4), 39-48.

[2] United Nations. (2019). The Global E-waste Monitor 2019. Retrieved from `https://www.itu.int/en/ITU-T/Workshops-and-Seminars/2019/Pages`

[3] Angwin, J., Larson, J., Mattu, S., & Kirchner, L. (2016). Machine Bias. *ProPublica*. Retrieved from `https://www.propublica.org/article/machine-bias-risk-assessmen`

The Legacy of Moore's Law

The End of Moore's Law?

Moore's Law, a term coined by Gordon Moore himself in 1965, posits that the number of transistors on a microchip doubles approximately every two years, leading to an exponential increase in computing power while simultaneously reducing relative cost. This observation has been the guiding principle of the semiconductor industry for decades, shaping not only technological advancements but also societal transformations. However, as we delve into the current landscape of computing, we must confront a pressing question: Is Moore's Law reaching its limits?

Theoretical Foundations of Moore's Law

At its core, Moore's Law is grounded in the principles of semiconductor physics and manufacturing technology. The law reflects the ability to miniaturize components and pack them more densely onto silicon chips. This miniaturization is driven by advancements in photolithography, materials science, and fabrication techniques. The fundamental equation that describes the relationship between transistor density N and time t can be expressed as:

$$N(t) = N_0 \cdot 2^{\frac{t}{T}}$$

where: - N_0 is the initial number of transistors, - T is the doubling time (approximately 2 years).

This exponential growth has led to remarkable increases in performance while keeping costs manageable. However, as we approach the physical limits of silicon-based technology, the question arises: Can this trend continue indefinitely?

Physical Limitations

The end of Moore's Law can be attributed to several physical limitations inherent in the materials and processes used in semiconductor manufacturing. As transistors shrink to the nanoscale, several phenomena emerge that challenge further miniaturization:

1. **Quantum Effects**: At extremely small scales, quantum tunneling becomes significant, where electrons can pass through barriers that would be insurmountable at larger scales. This can lead to increased leakage currents and reduced reliability of transistors.

2. **Heat Dissipation**: As transistor density increases, so does power consumption and heat generation. The inability to effectively dissipate heat can lead to thermal throttling, where performance is reduced to prevent damage.

3. **Variability**: As features shrink, the variability in manufacturing processes increases. This means that not all transistors behave identically, which can lead to unpredictable performance and reliability issues.

4. **Cost and Complexity**: The cost of developing new fabrication technologies has skyrocketed. The transition from 7nm to 5nm and beyond requires significant investments in new equipment and processes, raising questions about the economic viability of continued scaling.

Examples of Challenges in Scaling

To illustrate these challenges, consider the transition from 14nm to 10nm technology nodes. Intel faced significant delays and performance issues, which led to a reevaluation of their manufacturing roadmap. The difficulties encountered during this transition exemplify the broader industry trend of slowing progress in scaling down transistor sizes.

Furthermore, as companies like IBM and TSMC push the boundaries of semiconductor technology, they have begun exploring alternative materials such as graphene and transition metal dichalcogenides (TMDs) to circumvent some of the limitations of silicon. However, these materials are still in the experimental stages and not yet ready for mass production.

The Future Beyond Moore's Law

As the traditional scaling of transistors begins to plateau, the industry is shifting its focus towards new paradigms of computing that extend beyond the confines of Moore's Law. These include:

1. **Quantum Computing**: Leveraging the principles of quantum mechanics, quantum computers have the potential to perform certain calculations exponentially faster than classical computers. While still in their infancy, companies like Google and IBM are making strides in developing practical quantum systems.

2. **Neuromorphic Computing**: Inspired by the human brain, neuromorphic computing aims to create systems that mimic neural architectures. This approach could lead to more efficient processing for tasks such as machine learning and artificial intelligence.

3. **3D Integration**: Instead of continually shrinking transistors, researchers are exploring 3D chip architectures that stack multiple layers of circuits. This can significantly increase performance and reduce the distance data must travel, thus enhancing speed and efficiency.

4. **Specialized Processors**: As applications become more diverse, the demand for specialized processors (e.g., GPUs, TPUs) is growing. These chips are optimized for specific tasks, providing significant performance gains without relying solely on increasing transistor counts.

Conclusion

In conclusion, while Moore's Law has driven the semiconductor industry for over half a century, we are now witnessing the signs of its inevitable decline. Physical limitations, economic factors, and the emergence of new computing paradigms signal a shift in focus from sheer transistor count to innovative approaches that redefine what computing can achieve. As we look to the future, the legacy of Gordon Moore and his vision will undoubtedly continue to inspire new generations of technologists to explore uncharted territories in the realm of computing.

In Search of New Paradigms: Quantum Computing and Beyond

As we stand on the precipice of a new era in computing, the traditional frameworks that have guided the development of technology for decades are being challenged. Quantum computing, a field that harnesses the principles of quantum mechanics, promises to redefine our understanding of computation and its capabilities. In this section, we will explore the theoretical underpinnings of quantum computing, the challenges it presents, and the potential it holds for the future.

Theoretical Foundations of Quantum Computing

At the heart of quantum computing lies the concept of the **quantum bit** or **qubit.** Unlike classical bits, which can exist in one of two states (0 or 1), qubits can exist in a superposition of states. This characteristic allows quantum computers to process a vast amount of information simultaneously. Mathematically, a qubit can be represented as:

$$|\psi\rangle = \alpha|0\rangle + \beta|1\rangle$$

where $|\alpha|^2 + |\beta|^2 = 1$. Here, α and β are complex numbers that represent the probability amplitudes of the qubit being in the states $|0\rangle$ and $|1\rangle$, respectively.

Another critical principle of quantum computing is **entanglement.** When qubits become entangled, the state of one qubit becomes dependent on the state of another, regardless of the distance separating them. This phenomenon can be described by the following equation:

$$|\psi\rangle_{AB} = \frac{1}{\sqrt{2}} \left(|00\rangle + |11\rangle \right)$$

Entangled qubits can perform computations that would be infeasible for classical computers, leading to potentially exponential speedups in solving certain problems.

Challenges in Quantum Computing

Despite its promise, quantum computing faces several significant challenges. One of the most pressing issues is **decoherence,** which occurs when qubits lose their quantum state due to interactions with their environment. This process can be mathematically described using the **density matrix** formalism:

$$\rho(t) = e^{-\frac{t}{\tau}} \rho(0)$$

where τ is the coherence time of the qubit. Maintaining coherence long enough to perform meaningful computations is a critical hurdle that researchers are working to overcome.

Another challenge is the **error rates** associated with quantum operations. Quantum gates, the building blocks of quantum circuits, are prone to errors due to noise and imperfections in the physical systems. Error correction methods, such as the **surface code**, are being developed to mitigate these issues. The surface code is based on a lattice of qubits and allows for the correction of errors without measuring the qubits directly, which would collapse their quantum states.

Examples of Quantum Algorithms

Quantum computing has the potential to revolutionize various fields through specialized algorithms. One of the most notable examples is **Shor's algorithm**, which can factor large integers exponentially faster than the best-known classical algorithms. The mathematical formulation of Shor's algorithm involves quantum Fourier transforms and modular exponentiation, which can be expressed as:

$$\text{Period Finding: } f(x) = a^x \mod N$$

By efficiently finding the period of the function $f(x)$, Shor's algorithm can determine the prime factors of N in polynomial time, a task that is currently infeasible for classical computers when N is sufficiently large.

Another significant quantum algorithm is **Grover's algorithm**, which provides a quadratic speedup for unstructured search problems. The algorithm can be summarized by the following equation for the number of queries Q needed to find a target element in an unsorted database of size N:

$$Q = O(\sqrt{N})$$

This capability has profound implications for fields like cryptography, optimization, and database searching.

The Future of Quantum Computing

As we look to the future, the quest for new paradigms in computing is not limited to quantum mechanics alone. The integration of quantum computing with emerging technologies such as artificial intelligence and machine learning could lead to unprecedented advancements. For instance, quantum machine learning algorithms could process vast datasets far more efficiently than classical counterparts, enabling breakthroughs in fields ranging from drug discovery to climate modeling.

Furthermore, the exploration of **quantum supremacy**—the point at which quantum computers can solve problems that classical computers practically cannot—has already seen significant milestones. In 2019, Google claimed to achieve quantum supremacy with its 53-qubit processor, Sycamore, demonstrating the ability to perform a specific task in 200 seconds that would take the world's most powerful supercomputer approximately 10,000 years.

As we continue to push the boundaries of what is possible, the legacy of pioneers like Gordon Moore will guide our exploration into these new realms. The principles that underpin Moore's Law, which predicted the exponential growth of computing power, may evolve to accommodate the unique characteristics of quantum computing.

In conclusion, the journey into quantum computing represents a thrilling chapter in the evolution of technology. While significant challenges remain, the potential for transformative breakthroughs is immense. As we embrace this new paradigm, we stand on the brink of a revolution that could redefine our understanding of computation, information, and the very fabric of reality itself.

The Lasting Impact of Gordon Moore's Vision

Gordon Moore, co-founder of Intel Corporation, is not just a name; he is a cornerstone in the edifice of modern computing. His vision, encapsulated in what is now famously known as **Moore's Law**, has profoundly influenced the trajectory of technology and its integration into society. This section delves into the lasting impact of Moore's visionary insights, examining how his predictions have shaped the landscape of computing, propelled technological advancements, and fostered an environment of innovation that continues to resonate today.

Understanding Moore's Law

Moore's Law, formulated in 1965, posits that the number of transistors on a microchip doubles approximately every two years, leading to an exponential increase in computing power while simultaneously reducing relative costs. This observation not only highlighted the rapid pace of technological advancement but also set a benchmark for the semiconductor industry. The foundational equation that represents Moore's Law can be expressed as:

$$N(t) = N_0 \cdot 2^{\frac{t}{T}} \tag{36}$$

where:

+ $N(t)$ is the number of transistors at time t,

+ N_0 is the initial number of transistors,

+ T is the time period (typically two years),

+ t is the elapsed time.

This exponential growth has led to remarkable advancements in various fields, including personal computing, mobile technology, and artificial intelligence, making powerful computing accessible to the masses.

Transforming Industries

The implications of Moore's Law extend far beyond the realm of semiconductors. Industries such as healthcare, automotive, and entertainment have been transformed through the integration of advanced computing technologies. For instance, in healthcare, the ability to process vast amounts of data has led to breakthroughs in personalized medicine and genomics. The Human Genome Project, which mapped the entire human genome, was made feasible by the rapid advancements in computing power predicted by Moore's Law.

In the automotive industry, the emergence of autonomous vehicles is another testament to Moore's vision. The processing power required for real-time data analysis and decision-making in self-driving cars is a direct result of the exponential growth in computing capabilities. Companies like Tesla have leveraged this power to revolutionize transportation, showcasing how Moore's insights have catalyzed innovations that were once deemed impossible.

Fostering a Culture of Innovation

Moore's vision has also fostered a culture of innovation within the tech industry. The predictable advancements in computing power have encouraged companies to invest heavily in research and development, knowing that technological improvements will yield a competitive edge. This environment has led to the emergence of startups and tech giants alike, all vying to harness the power of increasingly capable computing systems.

For example, the rise of cloud computing services, such as Amazon Web Services (AWS) and Microsoft Azure, can be traced back to the principles laid out by Moore. The ability to scale computing resources dynamically and affordably has enabled businesses of all sizes to innovate without the heavy upfront costs traditionally associated with IT infrastructure.

Challenges and the Future of Moore's Law

Despite its profound impact, Moore's Law is facing challenges as physical limitations in semiconductor manufacturing begin to emerge. The miniaturization of transistors is approaching the atomic scale, raising concerns about the sustainability of continued exponential growth. As we approach these physical limits, the industry is exploring alternative computing paradigms, such as quantum computing and neuromorphic computing, which could redefine the future of technology.

$$\text{Quantum Speedup} = \frac{T_{\text{classical}}}{T_{\text{quantum}}} \tag{37}$$

This equation illustrates the potential speedup achievable through quantum algorithms compared to classical counterparts, emphasizing the need for new frameworks as Moore's Law reaches its limits.

Legacy and Continued Influence

The legacy of Gordon Moore is not merely confined to his law; it is reflected in the ethos of innovation and progress that permeates the tech industry. His insights have inspired generations of engineers, scientists, and entrepreneurs to push the boundaries of what is possible. The ongoing pursuit of faster, more efficient computing systems continues to be a driving force behind technological advancements, with Moore's vision serving as a guiding principle.

In conclusion, the lasting impact of Gordon Moore's vision is evident in the exponential growth of technology, the transformation of industries, and the culture of innovation that thrives today. As we stand on the precipice of new technological frontiers, Moore's contributions will undoubtedly continue to inspire and shape the future of computing for generations to come.

Moore's Law and the Evolution of Technology

Gordon Moore's observation, famously known as Moore's Law, has been a guiding principle in the semiconductor industry since its inception. Initially articulated in 1965, Moore predicted that the number of transistors on a microchip would double approximately every two years, leading to an exponential increase in computing power while simultaneously reducing costs. This observation was not merely a prediction but a reflection of the rapid advancements in technology that have characterized the industry over the last several decades.

Theoretical Underpinnings

At its core, Moore's Law is rooted in the principles of transistor scaling and miniaturization. As transistors become smaller, they can be packed more densely onto a chip, resulting in increased performance and efficiency. The relationship can be mathematically expressed as:

$$N(t) = N_0 \cdot 2^{\frac{t}{T}} \qquad (38)$$

where:

+ $N(t)$ is the number of transistors at time t,

+ N_0 is the initial number of transistors,

+ T is the doubling time (approximately 2 years), and

+ t is the elapsed time in years.

This exponential growth has led to significant advancements in various fields, including computing, telecommunications, and consumer electronics.

Practical Implications

The implications of Moore's Law extend beyond mere numbers. The increased transistor density has facilitated the development of more powerful processors, enabling complex computations that were once thought impossible. For example, the transition from the Intel 4004, which contained 2,300 transistors, to the Intel Core i9-11900K, boasting over 19 million transistors, exemplifies this exponential growth.

Furthermore, Moore's Law has driven innovation in software development. As hardware capabilities expand, software applications have become increasingly sophisticated, requiring more processing power and memory. This symbiotic relationship between hardware and software has accelerated advancements in artificial intelligence, machine learning, and data analytics, fundamentally altering industries and creating new markets.

Challenges and Limitations

Despite its historical accuracy, the continuation of Moore's Law faces significant challenges. As transistors approach atomic scales, physical limitations arise, including quantum tunneling and heat dissipation. These challenges raise questions about the sustainability of Moore's Law in the coming decades.

For instance, as the size of transistors shrinks below 5 nanometers, the behavior of electrons becomes unpredictable, leading to potential performance degradation. Researchers are exploring alternative materials, such as graphene and carbon nanotubes, to overcome these limitations, but practical implementations remain a work in progress.

Examples of Evolution Driven by Moore's Law

The evolution of technology driven by Moore's Law can be observed across various sectors:

+ **Personal Computing:** The shift from bulky desktop computers to sleek laptops and ultra-portable devices has been largely fueled by advancements in chip technology, allowing for greater performance in smaller form factors.

+ **Mobile Devices:** Smartphones, which integrate powerful processors capable of handling complex tasks, exemplify the impact of Moore's Law. The transition from 3G to 5G technology, enabling faster data transmission and improved connectivity, is also a direct consequence of advancements in semiconductor technology.

+ **Cloud Computing:** The rise of cloud computing services, such as Amazon Web Services and Microsoft Azure, relies heavily on the ability to deploy vast arrays of powerful microprocessors, made possible by Moore's Law. This has transformed how businesses operate, allowing for scalable and cost-effective solutions.

The Future Beyond Moore's Law

As we look to the future, the question arises: what comes after Moore's Law? Many experts believe that while the traditional scaling of transistors may slow, new paradigms will emerge. Quantum computing, neuromorphic computing, and advances in artificial intelligence are areas poised to redefine computing capabilities.

For example, quantum computers leverage the principles of quantum mechanics to process information in fundamentally different ways than classical computers. This could lead to breakthroughs in areas such as cryptography, materials science, and complex system modeling, which classical computers struggle to solve efficiently.

Conclusion

Moore's Law has been a cornerstone of technological evolution, shaping the landscape of the semiconductor industry and driving innovation across multiple domains. While challenges loom on the horizon, the spirit of exploration and ingenuity that Moore's Law embodies continues to inspire researchers and engineers alike. As we navigate the complexities of modern technology, it is clear that the legacy of Gordon Moore's vision will endure, paving the way for new frontiers in computing and beyond.

Personal Life: Behind the Scenes of a Genius

The Moore Family: A Supportive Foundation

The Love Story of Gordon and Betty Moore

The love story of Gordon and Betty Moore is not just a charming subplot in the narrative of a technological titan; it is a testament to the power of partnership in both personal and professional realms. Their bond, characterized by mutual respect, shared values, and a commitment to philanthropy, serves as an inspiring backdrop to Gordon Moore's monumental contributions to the semiconductor industry.

Gordon Moore first met Betty in the early 1950s at a social gathering in Palo Alto, California. At the time, Gordon was a young engineer at Fairchild Semiconductor, and Betty was a student at San Jose State University. Their initial connection was instantaneous, sparked by a shared love for science and innovation. As they conversed, it became clear that they were not just kindred spirits in their intellectual pursuits but also in their values and aspirations.

$$\text{Connection} = \text{Intellectual Curiosity} + \text{Shared Values} \qquad (39)$$

This equation encapsulates the essence of their relationship. Their intellectual curiosity drove them to explore the realms of technology and science together, while their shared values laid the foundation for a partnership built on trust and understanding.

After a whirlwind romance, Gordon proposed to Betty in 1956, and they married shortly thereafter. Their wedding was a modest affair, reflecting their humble beginnings and grounded nature. They settled into a life that balanced professional ambition with personal fulfillment, often supporting each other's endeavors. Betty, a talented artist, and Gordon, a burgeoning engineer, found ways

107

to intertwine their passions, creating a harmonious environment that fostered creativity and innovation.

As Gordon's career took off, so did Betty's commitment to supporting his work. She often accompanied him to industry events and conferences, where her keen insights and perspectives enriched the conversations. Betty's influence on Gordon's life was profound; she encouraged him to pursue his visions and ambitions, even when the path was fraught with uncertainty.

$$\text{Support} = \text{Encouragement} + \text{Understanding} \qquad (40)$$

This equation illustrates the dynamics of their relationship. Betty's unwavering support was characterized by her encouragement of Gordon's ambitions and her deep understanding of the challenges he faced in the rapidly evolving tech landscape.

The Moores' partnership extended beyond their personal lives into their professional endeavors. In 1968, when Gordon co-founded Intel with Robert Noyce, Betty played a crucial role in shaping the company's culture. She understood the importance of innovation and creativity in the tech industry and encouraged Gordon to foster an environment where ideas could flourish. This collaborative spirit was vital in the early days of Intel, as the company navigated the challenges of establishing itself in a competitive market.

Their shared commitment to philanthropy also defined their relationship. In 2000, the Moores established the Gordon and Betty Moore Foundation, which has since focused on environmental conservation, science, and patient care. Their philanthropic efforts reflect their belief in giving back to society and supporting causes that resonate with their values. Through the foundation, they have made significant contributions to various fields, including environmental science, science education, and health care.

$$\text{Impact} = \text{Philanthropy} \times \text{Shared Values} \qquad (41)$$

This equation highlights the Moores' commitment to making a difference in the world. Their philanthropic endeavors have had a lasting impact on countless lives, demonstrating how a shared vision can lead to meaningful change.

In their personal life, the Moores have always prioritized family. They raised two children, and their home was a nurturing environment that emphasized the importance of education, curiosity, and compassion. Gordon and Betty instilled in their children the values that guided their own lives, fostering a sense of responsibility and a desire to contribute positively to society.

As they navigated the ups and downs of life together, their relationship remained steadfast. They celebrated each other's successes and provided comfort during challenging times. Their love story is a beautiful example of how two individuals can complement each other, creating a partnership that thrives on collaboration and shared goals.

In conclusion, the love story of Gordon and Betty Moore is a remarkable narrative of partnership, support, and shared aspirations. Their bond has not only enriched their personal lives but has also significantly impacted the world through their professional achievements and philanthropic efforts. As we reflect on Gordon Moore's legacy, it is essential to recognize the integral role that Betty played in his journey, making their love story a vital chapter in the history of technology and innovation.

Raising a Family in the Midst of Technological Revolution

As the semiconductor industry began its meteoric rise in the 1960s and 1970s, Gordon Moore found himself not only at the helm of a technological revolution but also navigating the complexities of family life. The juxtaposition of groundbreaking advancements in technology and the nurturing of a family created a unique dynamic for Moore, who was determined to strike a balance between his professional commitments and personal responsibilities.

The Challenge of Time Management

In the early years of Intel, the demands on Moore's time were immense. The company was growing rapidly, and with it came the pressures of leadership, innovation, and competition. Moore often found himself working late nights and weekends, a common scenario for many executives in the fast-paced tech industry. However, he was acutely aware of the need to be present for his family.

To manage his time effectively, Moore adopted a strategic approach that involved prioritizing family activities and setting boundaries around work. He would often schedule family dinners and weekend outings, treating these commitments with the same seriousness as business meetings. This conscious effort to carve out family time provided a sense of stability and continuity amidst the chaos of a burgeoning tech empire.

The Influence of Betty Moore

Central to Moore's ability to balance work and family was the unwavering support of his wife, Betty Moore. Betty played a crucial role in creating a nurturing home environment, allowing Gordon to focus on his work without the constant worry of family obligations. Her commitment to their family was evident in her involvement with their children, ensuring that they felt loved and supported during the tumultuous years of their father's career.

Betty's influence extended beyond the home. She was actively engaged in community initiatives and philanthropic endeavors, fostering a culture of giving back that resonated with Gordon's values. Together, they instilled in their children the importance of education, hard work, and social responsibility—principles that would guide them throughout their lives.

Raising Children in a Tech-Centric World

As the Moores raised their children, they were acutely aware of the rapidly changing world around them. The advent of personal computing and the explosion of technology brought both opportunities and challenges. Moore and Betty encouraged their children to embrace technology while also fostering critical thinking and creativity.

The Moore household was filled with discussions about science, innovation, and ethics. Gordon often shared stories from his work at Intel, sparking curiosity and inspiring his children to explore their interests in STEM fields. This approach helped cultivate an environment where learning was valued, and the pursuit of knowledge was celebrated.

Balancing Innovation with Family Values

While the tech industry was often characterized by its relentless pursuit of innovation, the Moores remained grounded in their family values. They understood that technology should serve humanity, not the other way around. This philosophy guided their parenting style, as they emphasized the importance of empathy, ethics, and social responsibility in a world increasingly dominated by technology.

Moore's commitment to ethical leadership was reflected in his family life. He often discussed the implications of technological advancements with his children, encouraging them to think critically about the societal impacts of their choices. This dialogue not only prepared them for the future but also instilled a sense of responsibility to use their talents for the greater good.

Legacy of Family and Technology

As the years passed, the Moores witnessed firsthand the profound changes that technology brought to society. From the rise of the internet to the proliferation of mobile devices, each advancement presented new challenges and opportunities for their family. Through it all, Gordon and Betty remained steadfast in their commitment to each other and their children.

The legacy of raising a family amidst a technological revolution is evident in the lives of Moore's children, who have gone on to pursue successful careers in various fields. Their upbringing, marked by a balance of technological engagement and strong family values, has equipped them to navigate the complexities of the modern world.

In conclusion, raising a family in the midst of a technological revolution was a journey filled with challenges and triumphs for Gordon Moore. His ability to balance the demands of his career with the responsibilities of fatherhood is a testament to his dedication to both innovation and family. The Moore family's story serves as an inspiring example of how one can thrive in the fast-paced world of technology while remaining deeply connected to the values that matter most.

The Impact of Family on Moore's Career

Gordon Moore's career, marked by groundbreaking achievements and a legacy that transformed the semiconductor industry, was profoundly influenced by his family. The support of his loved ones provided the foundation upon which he built his professional life, navigating the complex interplay between personal commitments and the demands of a pioneering career in technology.

The Role of Betty Moore

At the heart of this familial influence was Betty Moore, Gordon's wife. Their partnership began in 1956, and it was characterized by mutual respect, shared values, and a deep understanding of each other's aspirations. Betty, who herself was an accomplished scientist, played a crucial role in supporting Gordon's ambitions. Her presence offered a stabilizing force during the tumultuous early years of Intel, a time when the company was evolving from a fledgling startup to a dominant player in the tech industry.

The emotional and intellectual partnership between Gordon and Betty can be likened to a dual-engine aircraft, where both engines must work in harmony to achieve flight. Betty's encouragement allowed Gordon to focus on his work, knowing that he had a steadfast partner at home. This balance between personal and professional life is often cited as essential for successful individuals, as it provides a safe harbor amid the storms of corporate challenges.

Raising a Family Amidst Technological Revolution

As Moore's career progressed, he and Betty welcomed two children, which added another layer of complexity to their lives. Raising a family during the rapid technological changes of the 1970s and 1980s presented both challenges and opportunities. The Moores instilled a sense of curiosity and a love for science in their children, reflecting Gordon's own upbringing. This nurturing environment fostered creativity and innovation, traits that would be invaluable in a household deeply intertwined with the world of technology.

The demands of a high-powered career often meant long hours and travel, but the Moores prioritized family time. Gordon's commitment to his family provided a grounding influence, allowing him to remain connected to the values that mattered most. This connection is evidenced by the family's involvement in philanthropic efforts, particularly through the Gordon and Betty Moore Foundation, which they established to support scientific research, environmental conservation, and patient care. Their joint commitment to giving back highlights how family values can shape professional endeavors and societal contributions.

Work-Life Balance: A Constant Challenge

The tech industry is notorious for its demanding work culture, often blurring the lines between professional obligations and personal life. For Moore, achieving a work-life balance was an ongoing challenge. The pressure to innovate and lead at Intel was immense, and the expectations of being a visionary in the semiconductor field often encroached on family time. However, the support of his family provided a buffer against the stresses of corporate life.

Moore's ability to compartmentalize his work and family life is a skill that many successful leaders strive to master. He recognized the importance of being present for his family, which not only strengthened their bonds but also contributed positively to his mental well-being. The love and support from his family allowed him to recharge and return to work with renewed vigor and creativity.

Legacy of Family Influence

The legacy of Gordon Moore's family influence extends beyond his immediate household. His children have taken up the mantle of philanthropy and scientific inquiry, embodying the values instilled in them by their parents. This generational transfer of values illustrates the profound impact that family can have on shaping the careers and aspirations of future leaders.

In summary, the impact of family on Gordon Moore's career cannot be overstated. The unwavering support of Betty Moore, the nurturing of their children, and the prioritization of family values created a solid foundation for his professional achievements. As Moore navigated the complexities of the tech industry, the influence of his family served as both a motivator and a source of strength, allowing him to leave an indelible mark on the world of computing while remaining grounded in the values that truly mattered.

$$\text{Career Success} = f(\text{Support, Balance, Values}) \qquad (42)$$

Where:

+ **Support** represents the emotional and practical backing from family.

+ **Balance** signifies the ability to manage work and personal life effectively.

+ **Values** encompasses the principles instilled by family that guide decision-making.

This equation encapsulates the essence of how family dynamics can significantly influence professional trajectories, particularly in high-stakes fields like technology and innovation.

Maintaining Work-Life Balance in the Tech Industry

In an industry characterized by rapid innovation and relentless competition, maintaining a healthy work-life balance can often feel like an elusive goal. For Gordon Moore, a pioneer in the semiconductor industry and co-founder of Intel, the challenge of balancing professional responsibilities with personal life was a recurring theme. This section explores the principles, challenges, and strategies that Moore employed to navigate the complexities of work-life balance in the tech industry.

The Importance of Work-Life Balance

The concept of work-life balance refers to the equilibrium between personal life and work commitments. It is essential for sustaining long-term productivity, reducing burnout, and enhancing overall well-being. Research indicates that professionals who achieve a favorable work-life balance are not only happier but also more engaged and productive at work. According to the National Institute for Occupational Safety and Health (NIOSH), work-related stress can lead to various health issues, including anxiety, depression, and cardiovascular diseases. Thus, balancing work and personal life is not merely a personal preference but a crucial aspect of maintaining mental and physical health.

Challenges in the Tech Industry

The tech industry presents unique challenges to achieving work-life balance. High-pressure environments, long hours, and the constant need for innovation can lead to an "always-on" culture. Employees may feel compelled to prioritize work over personal commitments, leading to stress and decreased job satisfaction. Moore himself experienced these pressures during Intel's formative years, where the demands of building a groundbreaking company often overshadowed personal time.

Example: The Intel Culture   Intel's early culture was one of intense dedication, where employees were often expected to work late hours and weekends to meet ambitious goals. This culture, while effective in driving innovation, raised concerns about employee well-being. Moore recognized the importance of fostering a supportive environment that encouraged balance. For instance, he implemented policies that promoted flexible working hours, allowing employees to manage their schedules more effectively.

Strategies for Achieving Balance

To combat the challenges of work-life balance, Moore employed several strategies that can serve as valuable lessons for current and future leaders in the tech industry.

1. Setting Boundaries   One of the most effective strategies for maintaining work-life balance is establishing clear boundaries between work and personal life. Moore emphasized the importance of setting specific work hours and sticking to them. This practice not only helps in managing time effectively but also signals to employees that personal time is valued.

2. Prioritizing Family   For Moore, family played a pivotal role in maintaining balance. He often made a conscious effort to prioritize family time, understanding that strong personal relationships contribute to overall happiness and fulfillment. By involving his family in his journey, he created a supportive network that helped him navigate the stresses of work.

3. **Encouraging Employee Well-Being** Moore believed that a healthy work environment is essential for productivity. He championed initiatives that promoted employee well-being, such as wellness programs, mental health resources, and team-building activities. These initiatives not only improved morale but also fostered a sense of community within the organization.

4. **Embracing Flexibility** In an industry where the pace of change is constant, flexibility is key. Moore advocated for flexible work arrangements that allowed employees to adapt their schedules based on personal needs. This approach not only reduced stress but also empowered employees to take ownership of their work-life balance.

The Role of Leadership

Leadership plays a crucial role in shaping organizational culture and influencing employees' ability to achieve work-life balance. Moore's leadership style was characterized by empathy and understanding. He recognized that his employees were not just cogs in a machine but individuals with lives outside of work. By fostering an inclusive environment that valued work-life balance, he set a precedent for future leaders in the tech industry.

Example: The Moore Family The support of Moore's family was instrumental in his success. His wife, Betty Moore, was not only a partner in life but also a collaborator in philanthropy and environmental initiatives. Their shared values and commitment to each other allowed Gordon to pursue his professional ambitions while ensuring that family remained a priority.

Conclusion

Maintaining work-life balance in the tech industry is an ongoing challenge that requires intentional effort from both individuals and leaders. Gordon Moore's journey provides valuable insights into the importance of setting boundaries, prioritizing family, promoting employee well-being, and embracing flexibility. By adopting these principles, current and future tech leaders can create a culture that supports work-life balance, ultimately leading to a more sustainable and productive workforce. As we navigate the complexities of modern work, the lessons from Moore's life remind us that success is not solely measured by professional achievements but also by the quality of our personal lives.

Hobbies and Passions Outside the Lab

Exploring the Great Outdoors: Moore's Love for Nature

Gordon Moore, a titan of technology, was not just a visionary in the realm of semiconductors; he was also a passionate lover of nature. This duality in his character played a significant role in shaping both his personal life and professional ethos. While the world recognized him for his groundbreaking contributions to computing, it was often the serenity of the outdoors that provided him with the inspiration and balance necessary to tackle the challenges of the tech industry.

A Retreat from the Digital World

In an era dominated by silicon and circuits, Moore found solace in the natural world. His love for the outdoors was more than a mere hobby; it was a refuge from the relentless pace of technological advancement. Whether it was hiking the rugged trails of the Sierra Nevada or sailing the pristine waters of the Pacific, Moore embraced the beauty of nature as a counterpoint to his high-tech life.

Moore's affinity for the outdoors can be traced back to his childhood in Pescadero, California, where the coastal landscape and the nearby redwood forests ignited his curiosity about the natural world. This early exposure instilled in him a profound appreciation for the environment, one that would later influence his philanthropic efforts and corporate responsibilities.

Nature as a Source of Inspiration

Moore often spoke of how time spent in nature rejuvenated his mind and sparked creativity. The tranquility of a forest or the rhythmic lapping of waves against a sailboat allowed him to clear his thoughts and approach problems with renewed vigor. This connection to the outdoors served as a fertile ground for ideas that would later manifest in his work at Intel.

For instance, during long sailing trips, Moore would contemplate the challenges facing the semiconductor industry. The vastness of the ocean and the unpredictability of the wind mirrored the dynamic landscape of technology, reminding him that innovation often requires navigating uncharted waters. The lessons learned from nature—adaptability, resilience, and harmony—became guiding principles in his leadership style.

Environmental Advocacy

Moore's love for nature extended beyond personal enjoyment; it evolved into a commitment to environmental stewardship. In 2000, he and his wife, Betty Moore, established the Gordon and Betty Moore Foundation, which has since dedicated significant resources to conservation efforts. The foundation's initiatives include protecting critical habitats, promoting sustainable agriculture, and supporting scientific research aimed at understanding and mitigating environmental challenges.

Moore's philanthropic efforts underscore a crucial point: the tech industry, while a driver of economic growth, must also take responsibility for its environmental impact. By advocating for sustainability, Moore sought to ensure that future generations could enjoy the natural wonders that had inspired him throughout his life.

Balancing Work and Leisure

In the fast-paced world of technology, finding a balance between work and leisure is often a challenge. Moore's dedication to outdoor activities served as a reminder of the importance of maintaining a well-rounded life. He understood that to foster innovation and creativity, one must also prioritize personal well-being.

For Moore, weekends were often spent hiking, sailing, or simply enjoying the beauty of the California coastline with family and friends. These moments of leisure not only provided a break from the demands of corporate life but also reinforced the value of collaboration and connection—principles that were central to his leadership at Intel.

Conclusion: A Legacy of Love for Nature

Gordon Moore's love for the great outdoors is a testament to the idea that true innovation is not solely born from the confines of a laboratory or a boardroom. Rather, it is often inspired by the natural world and the experiences we gather within it. As we reflect on his legacy, it is essential to recognize the profound impact that nature had on his life and work.

In a world increasingly defined by technology, Moore's commitment to environmental stewardship serves as a powerful reminder of our responsibility to protect the planet. His journey illustrates that the path to greatness is not just paved with technological triumphs but also enriched by a deep appreciation for the beauty and complexity of the world around us.

Sailing: Moore's Escape and Passion

Gordon Moore's life was not solely defined by his groundbreaking contributions to the semiconductor industry; it was also enriched by his passion for sailing. This hobby provided him with a unique escape from the high-pressure world of technology, allowing him to connect with nature while embracing the challenges of the open water. In this section, we will explore how sailing became an integral part of Moore's life, the lessons he learned from it, and how these experiences influenced his approach to innovation and leadership.

The Allure of the Sea

From an early age, Moore was drawn to the natural world, a fascination that only deepened as he grew older. The vastness of the ocean, the unpredictability of the weather, and the thrill of navigating through changing conditions captivated him. Sailing offered a perfect blend of adventure and tranquility, allowing him to escape the relentless pace of Silicon Valley.

Moore often described sailing as a meditative experience, where the complexities of life and work faded away. This connection with nature provided him with a sense of balance that was essential for a man whose career was marked by rapid technological advancements and intense competition. The rhythmic sound of the waves and the gentle sway of the boat became a sanctuary for his thoughts, often leading to moments of clarity and inspiration.

Lessons from the Water

Sailing is not merely a leisure activity; it is a discipline that requires skill, precision, and an understanding of the forces at play. Moore applied many of the lessons he learned on the water to his professional life.

1. Adaptability: Just as sailors must adjust their sails to changing winds, Moore learned the importance of adaptability in business. The tech industry is notorious for its rapid shifts, and those who can pivot quickly are often the ones who succeed. Moore's ability to embrace change and encourage his team to do the same was a hallmark of his leadership style.

2. Teamwork: Sailing often involves a crew working in unison to navigate the challenges of the sea. This experience taught Moore the value of collaboration. At Intel, he fostered a culture where teamwork was paramount, recognizing that the best ideas often emerged from diverse perspectives working together.

3. **Risk Management:**   The ocean can be unpredictable, and experienced sailors must assess risks continually.   Moore applied this principle to his business decisions, weighing potential rewards against possible pitfalls.   This analytical approach enabled him to make informed choices that propelled Intel to new heights.

4. **Patience and Persistence:**   Sailing requires patience; sometimes, the wind is not favorable, and progress is slow. Moore understood that success in technology often takes time and perseverance. His journey with Intel was not without its challenges, but his commitment to long-term goals kept him focused, even when immediate results were elusive.

Sailing Adventures and Competitions

Moore's passion for sailing extended beyond mere recreation; he participated in various sailing competitions, which further honed his skills and deepened his love for the sport. These adventures were not just about winning races; they were opportunities for personal growth and reflection.

One memorable competition was the *Transpacific Yacht Race*, a grueling event that tests sailors' endurance and tactical acumen. Moore's participation in such events underscored his belief in pushing boundaries, both personally and professionally.

Example: The Transpacific Yacht Race   The *Transpacific Yacht Race* is a biennial sailing race from Los Angeles to Honolulu, covering approximately 2,225 nautical miles. It is renowned for its challenging conditions, requiring sailors to navigate through unpredictable weather patterns and ocean currents.

The race exemplifies the spirit of adventure that Moore embodied. Just as he faced technological challenges at Intel, he confronted the vast Pacific Ocean's uncertainties. His experiences in such races reinforced his belief that success often lies beyond one's comfort zone.

Impact on Leadership and Innovation

Moore's sailing experiences profoundly influenced his leadership style at Intel. He often encouraged his team to embrace challenges and view obstacles as opportunities for growth. His philosophy mirrored the sailing mantra: *"It's not the destination; it's the journey."*

By fostering an environment where experimentation was encouraged, Moore empowered his employees to innovate without fear of failure. This approach led to groundbreaking advancements in microprocessor technology, as teams collaborated to navigate the complexities of development, much like a crew working together to sail a boat through turbulent waters.

Conclusion: The Legacy of Sailing in Moore's Life

In conclusion, sailing was more than a hobby for Gordon Moore; it was a vital part of his identity. The lessons he learned on the water—adaptability, teamwork, risk management, and patience—shaped his approach to leadership and innovation. As he navigated the complexities of the tech world, the ocean remained a constant source of inspiration and solace.

Moore's legacy is not only defined by his monumental contributions to technology but also by the values he cultivated through his love for sailing. By embracing the spirit of adventure and the importance of collaboration, he left an indelible mark on the industry and inspired future generations to navigate their own journeys with courage and creativity.

Philanthropy and Giving Back

Gordon Moore's legacy extends far beyond the realm of semiconductors and microprocessors; it is also deeply rooted in his commitment to philanthropy and giving back to society. As a visionary leader, Moore recognized the importance of using his wealth and influence to address pressing global issues, particularly in education, environmental conservation, and scientific research. This section explores the various dimensions of Moore's philanthropic endeavors, illustrating how he has sought to make a meaningful impact on the world.

The Moore Foundation: A Legacy of Giving

In 2000, Gordon and his wife, Betty Moore, established the **Gordon and Betty Moore Foundation**, which has since become a significant force in philanthropy. With an endowment of approximately $5 billion, the foundation focuses on four key areas: *Environmental Conservation, Science, Patient Care,* and *San Francisco Bay Area Community.* The foundation's mission is to create positive outcomes through rigorous scientific research, innovative partnerships, and strategic grant-making.

Environmental Conservation

One of the foundation's primary focuses is environmental conservation. The Moores have funded numerous initiatives aimed at preserving biodiversity, promoting sustainable practices, and combating climate change. For instance, the foundation has invested in projects that protect critical ecosystems, such as the *Amazon rainforest* and the *Coral Triangle*. These efforts are grounded in the belief that a healthy planet is essential for future generations.

$$\text{Biodiversity Loss} = (\text{Habitat Destruction} + \text{Pollution} + \text{Climate Change}) \times (\text{Human Impa}$$
$$(43)$$

The equation above illustrates the complex interplay of factors contributing to biodiversity loss, which the Moore Foundation aims to mitigate through its conservation programs.

Advancing Scientific Research

Moore's passion for science is evident in the foundation's commitment to advancing scientific research. The foundation funds various research initiatives, including those focused on *quantum computing, genomics,* and *environmental science.* By supporting groundbreaking research, the foundation seeks to foster innovation that can lead to transformative solutions for global challenges.

For example, the foundation has invested in the *Moore Inventor Fellows program,* which supports early-career inventors who are developing innovative solutions to pressing problems. This initiative not only provides financial support but also fosters a community of like-minded individuals dedicated to making a difference.

Education: Empowering Future Generations

Education is another cornerstone of the Moore Foundation's philanthropic efforts. The foundation invests in initiatives that enhance science education and promote STEM (Science, Technology, Engineering, and Mathematics) learning. By empowering the next generation of scientists and innovators, Moore aims to ensure a future where technological advancements continue to thrive.

One notable initiative is the *California Science Center,* which provides hands-on science education to students and educators. The center aims to inspire curiosity and a love for science, fostering a new generation of thinkers and problem solvers.

Community Engagement and Support

Beyond environmental and scientific initiatives, the Moore Foundation is also dedicated to supporting local communities, particularly in the San Francisco Bay Area. The foundation provides grants to organizations that address critical social issues, such as *homelessness*, *education*, and *healthcare*. By investing in community-driven solutions, the foundation seeks to create lasting change and improve the quality of life for residents.

$$\text{Community Well-Being} = (\text{Education} + \text{Healthcare} + \text{Economic Opportunities}) \div (\text{S} \quad (44)$$

This equation highlights the importance of addressing multiple facets of community well-being to achieve sustainable improvements.

The Impact of Philanthropy on Moore's Legacy

Gordon Moore's philanthropic efforts have not only made a significant impact on various global challenges but have also set a precedent for other tech leaders. His commitment to giving back serves as an inspiration for others in the industry to leverage their resources for the greater good. Moore's legacy is a reminder that success is not solely measured by financial achievements, but also by the positive impact one can have on society.

In conclusion, Gordon Moore's philanthropy reflects his belief in the power of science, education, and community engagement to create a better world. Through the Gordon and Betty Moore Foundation, he has demonstrated that the responsibility of innovation extends beyond the laboratory and into the broader society. As we look to the future, Moore's commitment to philanthropy serves as a guiding principle for those who aspire to make a difference in the world.

Finding Joy and Inspiration Outside of Technology

In the fast-paced world of technology, where innovation often eclipses personal pursuits, Gordon Moore found solace and inspiration in the natural world and his hobbies. This section explores how Moore's engagement with activities outside the realm of semiconductors not only provided a necessary balance to his life but also fueled his creativity and problem-solving abilities in his professional endeavors.

The Great Outdoors: A Source of Renewal

Moore's affinity for nature was not merely a pastime; it was a fundamental aspect of his identity. Growing up in the picturesque coastal town of Pescadero, California, he developed an early appreciation for the environment. This connection to nature became a sanctuary for Moore, offering a respite from the pressures of corporate life.

Research indicates that spending time in natural settings can enhance cognitive function and creativity. A study by Berman et al. (2008) demonstrated that individuals who walked in nature performed better on cognitive tasks than those who walked in urban environments. Moore's frequent hikes and excursions into the wilderness could be seen as a practical application of this theory, allowing him to recharge mentally and emotionally.

Sailing: The Art of Navigation and Strategy

Another significant passion for Moore was sailing. He often spent weekends on the water, navigating the winds and tides. Sailing is an activity that requires not only physical skill but also strategic thinking and foresight—qualities that Moore applied in his professional life at Intel.

The act of sailing mirrors many aspects of leadership in technology: one must navigate uncertain waters, adjust to changing conditions, and make quick decisions based on incomplete information. Moore's experiences on the water taught him the importance of adaptability and resilience, traits that are essential in both sailing and technology.

$$\text{Velocity} = \frac{\text{Distance}}{\text{Time}} \tag{45}$$

The above equation exemplifies the importance of speed and efficiency in sailing, which parallels Moore's approach to innovation. Just as a sailor must optimize their route to reach their destination, Moore sought to streamline processes and foster innovation at Intel.

Philanthropy: Giving Back to the Community

Moore's commitment to philanthropy also played a significant role in his life outside of technology. Through the Gordon and Betty Moore Foundation, he championed causes related to environmental conservation, science education, and patient care. This philanthropic endeavor was not just an act of giving; it was a manifestation of his values and a way to inspire future generations.

The foundation's focus on environmental sustainability aligns with Moore's love for nature. By investing in projects that protect ecosystems and promote scientific research, he ensured that his legacy extended beyond the semiconductor industry. The foundation has funded numerous initiatives, including the creation of marine protected areas and support for innovative scientific research.

Finding Balance: The Interplay Between Work and Play

Moore's ability to find joy outside of his work was essential for maintaining a healthy work-life balance. In an industry that often demands long hours and constant connectivity, he recognized the importance of stepping back and engaging in activities that brought him joy.

Studies have shown that a balanced lifestyle contributes to greater job satisfaction and productivity. For instance, the American Psychological Association (APA) has found that employees who engage in leisure activities report lower stress levels and higher overall well-being. Moore's commitment to sailing, hiking, and philanthropy not only enriched his personal life but also enhanced his effectiveness as a leader.

Conclusion: The Holistic Approach to Life and Work

In conclusion, Gordon Moore's life outside of technology was marked by a deep appreciation for nature, a passion for sailing, and a commitment to philanthropy. These pursuits provided him with joy, inspiration, and a sense of purpose that complemented his groundbreaking work in the semiconductor industry. By finding balance in his life, Moore exemplified the idea that personal fulfillment and professional success are not mutually exclusive but rather intertwined facets of a well-rounded existence.

As we reflect on Moore's legacy, it is clear that his ability to find inspiration outside of technology was integral to his success. It serves as a reminder to all of us that while we may be driven by our careers, it is the moments spent in nature, the connections we foster, and the joy we find in our passions that truly enrich our lives.

The Lasting Legacy of Gordon Moore

Awards, Honors, and Recognition

Gordon Moore's contributions to the semiconductor industry and technology at large have not gone unnoticed. Over the years, he has been the recipient of numerous prestigious awards and honors that reflect his profound impact on the field of electronics, computing, and beyond. This section delves into the accolades that celebrate Moore's legacy and his role in shaping the modern technological landscape.

National Medal of Technology and Innovation

In 1990, Gordon Moore was awarded the National Medal of Technology and Innovation, one of the highest honors bestowed upon American inventors and innovators. This award recognizes individuals who have made significant contributions to the advancement of technology in the United States. Moore's receipt of this medal was a testament to his groundbreaking work in semiconductors and his visionary insights that led to the development of microprocessors. The citation accompanying the award specifically highlighted his role in co-founding Intel Corporation and his pioneering work on Moore's Law, which predicts the exponential growth of transistor density on integrated circuits.

IEEE Medal of Honor

In 2002, Moore received the IEEE Medal of Honor, awarded by the Institute of Electrical and Electronics Engineers (IEEE). This prestigious accolade is given to individuals who have made extraordinary contributions to the field of electrical and electronics engineering. Moore was recognized for his pivotal role in the development of the semiconductor industry and for his leadership at Intel. The IEEE Medal of Honor is a symbol of excellence, and Moore's receipt of it underscores his status as a leading figure in the engineering community.

Silicon Valley Engineering Hall of Fame

Moore's influence extends beyond individual awards; he was inducted into the Silicon Valley Engineering Hall of Fame in 2004. This recognition honors engineers who have made a significant impact on the technological landscape of Silicon Valley, a region synonymous with innovation. Moore's induction serves as a reminder of his foundational role in establishing Silicon Valley as a global center for technology and entrepreneurship. His work at Intel and his vision for the future of computing have left an indelible mark on the industry.

The Computer History Museum's Fellow Award

In 2007, the Computer History Museum honored Moore with its Fellow Award, recognizing his contributions to the computing revolution. The museum celebrates individuals whose innovations have significantly impacted the evolution of computing technology. Moore's insights into the scalability of integrated circuits and his predictions regarding the future of computing have been instrumental in shaping the industry. The award highlights his role not only as a pioneer but also as a thought leader who foresaw the potential of computing technology.

Honorary Doctorates

Moore has also been the recipient of several honorary doctorates from esteemed institutions, acknowledging his contributions to science and technology. Notably, he received an honorary Doctor of Science and Engineering degree from the University of California, Berkeley, in 1998. This honor reflects his deep connection to the university, where he began his academic journey and laid the groundwork for his future innovations.   Such recognitions from academic institutions underscore the importance of Moore's work in inspiring future generations of engineers and scientists.

The Moore Foundation and Philanthropic Recognition

Beyond his technical achievements, Moore's philanthropic efforts through the Gordon and Betty Moore Foundation have also garnered recognition. Established in 2000, the foundation focuses on environmental conservation, science, and patient care, reflecting Moore's commitment to giving back to society.   The foundation has funded numerous initiatives aimed at advancing scientific research and promoting sustainability. Moore's philanthropic work has been acknowledged through various awards that celebrate his dedication to improving the world through innovation and responsible stewardship.

Legacy and Lasting Impact

The awards and honors received by Gordon Moore are not merely accolades; they represent a legacy of innovation and leadership that continues to inspire. Moore's vision has fundamentally changed the way we interact with technology, and his contributions have paved the way for advancements that have transformed industries and everyday life. As we reflect on the accolades he has received, it becomes clear that Moore's influence extends far beyond the confines of the semiconductor industry; it resonates through the very fabric of modern society.

In conclusion, the recognition that Gordon Moore has received throughout his career serves as a testament to his unparalleled contributions to technology and society. From the National Medal of Technology and Innovation to his induction into various halls of fame, each award encapsulates a facet of his remarkable journey—a journey that has not only revolutionized the world of computing but has also left a lasting imprint on generations to come. Moore's legacy is a beacon for aspiring innovators, reminding us all of the power of vision, perseverance, and an unyielding commitment to excellence in the pursuit of knowledge and progress.

The Moore Auditorium: A Tribute to a Visionary

The Moore Auditorium stands as a testament to the enduring legacy of Gordon Moore, not just as a pioneer of the semiconductor industry but as a visionary whose impact transcends the boundaries of technology. Located at the heart of the Stanford University campus, the auditorium is more than just a venue for lectures and events; it embodies the spirit of innovation and collaboration that Moore championed throughout his life.

A Space for Inspiration

The design of the Moore Auditorium reflects the principles of openness and accessibility that Moore valued. With a seating capacity of over 300, it is equipped with state-of-the-art audiovisual technology, enabling it to host a variety of events ranging from academic conferences to community discussions. The auditorium's architecture is characterized by clean lines and a modern aesthetic, symbolizing the forward-thinking ethos that Moore embodied.

$$V = A \cdot h \tag{46}$$

Where V is the volume of the auditorium, A is the area of the base, and h is the height. The spacious design allows for optimal acoustics and sightlines, ensuring that every voice can be heard and every idea can be shared.

Celebrating Innovation

The Moore Auditorium is not merely a physical space; it serves as a hub for innovation and collaboration. Regularly, it hosts lectures and panels featuring thought leaders in technology, science, and entrepreneurship. These events foster a culture of dialogue and exploration, encouraging attendees to think critically about the future of technology and its implications for society.

For example, in 2022, the auditorium hosted a symposium on "The Future of Quantum Computing," bringing together leading researchers and industry experts to discuss the challenges and opportunities in this rapidly evolving field. The discussions highlighted the importance of interdisciplinary collaboration, a value that Moore consistently promoted throughout his career.

Educational Initiatives

In addition to hosting events, the Moore Auditorium plays a crucial role in educational initiatives aimed at inspiring the next generation of innovators. The auditorium is often used for workshops and seminars aimed at students, providing them with the opportunity to engage with cutting-edge research and learn from experts in the field.

One noteworthy program is the "Moore Scholars Initiative," which offers mentorship and resources to aspiring young scientists and engineers. This initiative not only honors Moore's legacy but also ensures that his commitment to education and innovation continues to thrive.

$$S = \sum_{i=1}^{n} \frac{1}{i^2} \tag{47}$$

This equation, representing the Riemann zeta function at $s = 2$, serves as a reminder of the beauty and complexity of mathematics, a field that Moore deeply appreciated. The auditorium frequently features talks that explore the intersection of mathematics, computer science, and engineering, illustrating the foundational role these disciplines play in technological advancement.

Community Engagement

The Moore Auditorium also serves as a venue for community engagement, bridging the gap between academia and the public. Events such as "Tech Talks for the Community" invite local residents to learn about the latest advancements in technology and how they can impact daily life. This initiative reflects Moore's belief in the importance of making technology accessible and understandable to everyone.

For instance, in a recent event titled "Understanding Artificial Intelligence," experts discussed the implications of AI on society, addressing both its potential benefits and ethical concerns. The interactive format of the event encouraged participants to ask questions and engage in meaningful dialogue, exemplifying the auditorium's role as a platform for community discourse.

A Lasting Legacy

The establishment of the Moore Auditorium is a fitting tribute to a man whose vision and leadership transformed the world of technology. It stands as a beacon of inspiration for current and future generations, reminding us of the importance of innovation, collaboration, and ethical responsibility in the ever-evolving landscape of technology.

As we look to the future, the Moore Auditorium will continue to play a pivotal role in shaping the discourse around technology and its impact on society. In an era where the pace of technological advancement is accelerating, spaces like the Moore Auditorium are essential for fostering the conversations that will guide us toward a more equitable and sustainable future.

$$Legacy = Innovation + Education + Community \qquad (48)$$

This equation encapsulates the essence of Gordon Moore's contributions and the principles that the Moore Auditorium embodies. It serves not only as a tribute to a visionary but as a catalyst for continued exploration and discovery in the realms of science and technology.

The Impact of Moore's Leadership on Future Generations

Gordon Moore's leadership at Intel not only reshaped the landscape of the semiconductor industry but also set the stage for future generations of engineers, scientists, and entrepreneurs. His visionary approach, encapsulated in what has come to be known as **Moore's Law**, has influenced not just technological advancement but also the ethos of innovation and entrepreneurship in the tech sector.

Inspiration for Innovation

Moore's Law, which posits that the number of transistors on a microchip doubles approximately every two years, has been a guiding principle for the semiconductor industry since its inception. This exponential growth has not only driven down costs but also fueled an unprecedented pace of innovation. The implications of Moore's Law extend beyond mere numbers; it has inspired generations of engineers to push the boundaries of what is possible.

For instance, the rapid advancements in computing power have enabled the development of artificial intelligence (AI), machine learning, and big data analytics. These fields, which rely heavily on the foundational technologies established during Moore's era, have transformed industries ranging from healthcare to finance. The ability to process vast amounts of data quickly and efficiently has opened new avenues for research and development, demonstrating the far-reaching impact of Moore's leadership.

$$N(t) = N_0 \cdot 2^{\frac{t}{T}} \qquad (49)$$

Where: - $N(t)$ is the number of transistors at time t, - N_0 is the initial number of transistors, - T is the time period (typically two years).

This equation illustrates the exponential growth that has characterized the semiconductor industry, a phenomenon that has become a cornerstone of modern technology.

Cultivating a Culture of Collaboration

Under Moore's leadership, Intel became synonymous with collaboration and innovation. He fostered an environment where ideas could flourish, encouraging cross-disciplinary teamwork that brought together experts from various fields. This collaborative spirit has had a lasting impact on future generations, teaching them the importance of diverse perspectives in solving complex problems.

For example, the collaboration between hardware engineers and software developers at Intel led to the creation of optimized systems that are still in use today. This model of interdisciplinary cooperation has been adopted by many tech companies, promoting a culture where innovation is not confined to a single department but is a collective endeavor.

Ethical Leadership and Responsibility

Moore's leadership also emphasized the importance of ethical considerations in technology development. As the tech industry grew, so did the ethical dilemmas surrounding issues such as privacy, data security, and environmental impact. Moore's commitment to corporate responsibility and philanthropy set a precedent for future leaders in technology.

The establishment of the **Gordon and Betty Moore Foundation** is a testament to his belief in giving back to society. The foundation focuses on environmental conservation, science, and patient care, illustrating how leaders in technology can influence positive change beyond their immediate industry. Future generations of tech leaders are inspired to think critically about the societal implications of their innovations, ensuring that technological progress aligns with ethical standards.

Mentorship and Legacy

Moore's impact on future generations is also evident in his role as a mentor. Many of Intel's leaders, including Andy Grove and Paul Otellini, credit Moore's guidance and vision as instrumental in their own careers. This mentorship culture has cultivated a new generation of leaders who prioritize innovation, collaboration, and ethical responsibility.

For example, Andy Grove's leadership at Intel was heavily influenced by Moore's principles. Grove's focus on strategic planning and operational excellence helped Intel navigate challenges in the rapidly evolving tech landscape, ensuring the company's continued success. This legacy of mentorship continues to shape the careers of young professionals in the tech industry, encouraging them to adopt a holistic approach to leadership.

Educational Influence

Moore's legacy extends into education as well. By emphasizing the importance of science and engineering, he has inspired countless students to pursue careers in technology. Initiatives like the **Moore Foundation's Education Program** aim to enhance science education and foster a new generation of innovators.

Programs funded by the foundation have focused on improving STEM (Science, Technology, Engineering, and Mathematics) education, ensuring that students are equipped with the skills necessary to thrive in a technology-driven world. This commitment to education reflects Moore's understanding that the future of technology relies on the next generation of thinkers and problem solvers.

Conclusion

In conclusion, Gordon Moore's leadership has had a profound and lasting impact on future generations. His visionary approach, emphasis on collaboration, commitment to ethical leadership, and focus on education have created a legacy that continues to inspire innovation in the technology sector. As we look to the future, the principles established by Moore will undoubtedly guide the next wave of technological advancements, ensuring that the spirit of innovation he championed lives on.

The enduring influence of Moore's leadership serves as a reminder of the responsibility that comes with technological power. Future generations of leaders in the tech industry are tasked with not only advancing technology but also ensuring that their innovations contribute positively to society. As they navigate the challenges and opportunities that lie ahead, they carry with them the lessons learned from one of the most influential figures in the history of technology.

Carrying Forward Moore's Vision and Values

Gordon Moore's legacy extends far beyond the boundaries of silicon chips and microprocessors; it encompasses a profound vision for the future of technology and its role in society. As we navigate the complexities of the modern world, the principles and values that Moore championed continue to resonate, guiding current and future generations of innovators, technologists, and leaders.

Emphasizing Innovation and Creativity

At the heart of Moore's vision is an unwavering commitment to innovation. He believed that technological advancement should not only be about enhancing performance but also about fostering creativity and solving real-world problems. This ethos is encapsulated in the concept of **disruptive innovation**, which refers to innovations that create new markets and value networks, ultimately displacing established market leaders and products.

For example, the rise of cloud computing exemplifies this principle. Originally, computing resources were confined to physical servers, but with the advent of cloud technology, companies can now access scalable resources on demand, fundamentally changing how businesses operate. This shift has enabled startups to compete with established giants, democratizing access to powerful computing capabilities and fostering a new wave of innovation.

Sustainability and Ethical Responsibility

Another cornerstone of Moore's vision is the importance of sustainability and ethical responsibility in technology development. As the world grapples with climate change and environmental degradation, Moore's values prompt us to consider the ecological impact of our technological pursuits. The semiconductor industry, while pivotal in advancing technology, also faces scrutiny over its environmental footprint.

Moore's commitment to sustainability is reflected in initiatives such as the **Moore Foundation**, which actively supports environmental causes and promotes research in sustainable practices. Companies are now encouraged to adopt **green technology** practices, such as energy-efficient manufacturing processes and sustainable sourcing of materials. An example of this is Intel's investment in renewable energy sources, aiming to power its facilities with 100% renewable energy, demonstrating that profitability and environmental stewardship can coexist.

Fostering Education and Collaboration

Moore's vision also emphasizes the importance of education and collaboration in advancing technology. He understood that the future of innovation relies heavily on nurturing talent and fostering a collaborative environment. This is particularly relevant in an era where interdisciplinary approaches are essential for tackling complex challenges.

Programs that promote **STEM education** (Science, Technology, Engineering, and Mathematics) are vital in this regard. Initiatives like *Code.org* and *Girls Who Code* aim to inspire and equip the next generation of technologists, ensuring a diverse pool of talent ready to innovate. Furthermore, collaborations between academia, industry, and government can catalyze breakthroughs that address societal needs. For instance, partnerships between universities and tech companies have led to advancements in artificial intelligence and machine learning, fields that are reshaping industries from healthcare to finance.

Encouraging Ethical Leadership

As technology continues to evolve, the role of ethical leadership becomes increasingly critical. Moore's values remind us that with great power comes great responsibility. Leaders in the tech industry must prioritize ethical considerations in their decision-making processes, ensuring that technological advancements do not come at the expense of societal welfare.

The concept of **ethical AI** has gained traction as artificial intelligence becomes more integrated into our lives. Leaders are challenged to create frameworks that guide the responsible use of AI, addressing issues such as bias, privacy, and accountability. Companies like Google and Microsoft have established AI ethics boards to oversee their developments, reflecting Moore's belief in the necessity of ethical oversight in technological innovation.

The Legacy of Moore's Law

While Moore's Law— the observation that the number of transistors on a microchip doubles approximately every two years— has driven exponential growth in computing power, its implications extend beyond mere numbers. The law serves as a reminder of the relentless pace of technological advancement and the need to adapt continuously.

As we look to the future, the challenge lies in finding new paradigms that will sustain this growth. Quantum computing, for instance, represents a potential successor to classical computing paradigms, promising to solve problems deemed intractable by current technologies. By embracing the spirit of Moore's Law, innovators are encouraged to explore uncharted territories, pushing the boundaries of what is possible.

Conclusion

Carrying forward Gordon Moore's vision and values requires a multifaceted approach that prioritizes innovation, sustainability, education, ethical leadership, and a commitment to exploring new frontiers. As we stand on the precipice of technological advancement, it is imperative that we honor Moore's legacy by striving to create a future where technology serves humanity, enhances our quality of life, and addresses the pressing challenges of our time. In doing so, we not only pay tribute to a visionary leader but also pave the way for a brighter, more equitable future for generations to come.

Conclusion

Gordon Moore: The Man, the Visionary, the Legend

The Unfiltered Intel Revolution and Its Enduring Impact

The journey of Gordon Moore and the rise of Intel Corporation is not merely a tale of technological advancement; it is a narrative that encapsulates the very essence of innovation, ambition, and the relentless pursuit of progress. Moore's vision, articulated through what has come to be known as **Moore's Law**, has shaped the trajectory of the semiconductor industry and the broader landscape of computing.

Understanding Moore's Law

At its core, Moore's Law posits that the number of transistors on a microchip doubles approximately every two years, leading to a corresponding increase in computing power and a decrease in relative cost. This exponential growth can be mathematically represented as:

$$N(t) = N_0 \times 2^{\frac{t}{T}} \tag{50}$$

where: - $N(t)$ is the number of transistors at time t, - N_0 is the initial number of transistors, - T is the time period (typically two years) for the doubling effect.

The implications of Moore's Law are profound. It has not only driven the rapid advancement of technology but has also influenced economic models, manufacturing processes, and consumer expectations. The expectation that technology will continue to improve at an exponential rate has led to a culture of innovation that permeates the tech industry.

The Intel Revolution

Intel's founding in 1968 by Gordon Moore and Robert Noyce marked the beginning of a new era in computing. The company's early success with the Intel 4004, the first commercially available microprocessor, set the stage for a revolution in personal computing. The microprocessor was a game-changer, allowing for the miniaturization of computing devices and paving the way for the development of personal computers.

The introduction of subsequent microprocessors, such as the Intel 8008 and 8080, further solidified Intel's dominance in the market. These innovations were not simply incremental improvements; they were transformative, enabling a wave of technological advancements that would redefine how individuals and businesses interacted with technology.

The Broader Impact of Intel's Innovations

Intel's influence extends beyond its products. The company has played a pivotal role in the establishment of the semiconductor industry as a cornerstone of the global economy. The proliferation of microprocessors has enabled advancements in various fields, including telecommunications, healthcare, and entertainment.

For instance, the advent of personal computing revolutionized the workplace, allowing for greater productivity and the emergence of new industries. Software applications, which rely heavily on the capabilities of microprocessors, have transformed everyday tasks, from accounting to graphic design.

Moreover, Intel's commitment to research and development has fostered a culture of innovation that has inspired countless startups and tech companies around the world. The company's approach to fostering talent and encouraging creativity has led to breakthroughs in artificial intelligence, machine learning, and quantum computing.

Challenges and Ethical Considerations

Despite its successes, the Intel revolution has not been without challenges. The rapid pace of innovation has raised ethical questions regarding the environmental impact of semiconductor manufacturing, labor practices, and the responsibility of tech companies in addressing societal issues.

The **Moore Foundation**, established by Gordon Moore and his wife, Betty, emphasizes philanthropy and environmental sustainability. The foundation's initiatives reflect Moore's commitment to balancing technological advancement with social responsibility. For example, their focus on environmental activism highlights the importance of sustainable practices in the tech industry.

Legacy and Future Directions

As we reflect on the enduring impact of the Intel revolution, it is essential to acknowledge that Moore's Law is not merely a prediction of technological growth; it is a testament to the vision and ingenuity of individuals like Gordon Moore. The legacy of his contributions continues to influence the direction of technology, inspiring future generations of innovators to push the boundaries of what is possible.

In conclusion, the unfiltered Intel revolution represents a paradigm shift in how we perceive and interact with technology. It has laid the foundation for the modern digital age, and its effects will be felt for decades to come. As we look to the future, the challenge will be to harness the power of innovation responsibly, ensuring that the benefits of technology are accessible to all while addressing the ethical dilemmas that arise in an ever-evolving landscape.

Epilogue

The Future of Computing: Moore's Prediction Revisited

The Evolution of Technology Beyond Moore's Law

Gordon Moore's observation that the number of transistors on a microchip doubles approximately every two years, commonly known as Moore's Law, has been a guiding principle in the semiconductor industry since its inception. However, as we venture further into the 21st century, the limitations of this law are becoming increasingly apparent. The exponential growth predicted by Moore's Law is facing significant physical, technological, and economic challenges, prompting a search for new paradigms in computing technology.

Physical Limitations

As transistors shrink to nanoscale dimensions, we encounter fundamental physical limitations that challenge the continuation of Moore's Law. The primary issues include:

+ **Quantum Tunneling:** As transistors reach sizes on the order of 5 nanometers, electrons can tunnel through the barriers meant to contain them, leading to leakage currents that can cause devices to malfunction. This phenomenon is described by the quantum mechanical principle of tunneling, where particles have a probability of crossing potential barriers despite not having enough energy to do so classically.

+ **Heat Dissipation:** Smaller transistors generate heat due to increased electrical activity and reduced thermal dissipation capabilities. This heat can lead to thermal runaway, where rising temperatures cause further increases in current, potentially damaging the chip. The relationship between power dissipation P, voltage V, and current I can be expressed as:

$$P = V \cdot I$$

As transistor counts increase, managing heat becomes a critical issue for maintaining performance and reliability.

+ **Diminished Returns:** As we push the limits of transistor scaling, the performance gains per transistor have begun to plateau. The economic viability of producing smaller chips diminishes as the cost of fabrication increases while performance improvements do not keep pace.

New Computing Paradigms

In light of these challenges, researchers and technologists are exploring alternative computing paradigms that could potentially replace or complement traditional silicon-based computing. Some of these paradigms include:

+ **Quantum Computing:** Quantum computers leverage the principles of quantum mechanics to perform calculations at speeds unattainable by classical computers. Utilizing qubits, which can exist in multiple states simultaneously, quantum computers can solve complex problems, such as factoring large numbers or simulating quantum systems, much faster than classical counterparts. The fundamental operation of a quantum gate can be represented as:

$$|\psi\rangle = U|\phi\rangle$$

where U is a unitary operator acting on the quantum state $|\phi\rangle$.

+ **Neuromorphic Computing:** This approach mimics the neural structure and functioning of the human brain, using artificial neurons and synapses to process information in a more energy-efficient manner. Neuromorphic chips can perform tasks such as pattern recognition and sensory processing with lower power consumption compared to traditional architectures. The behavior of a simple neuron can be modeled by the equation:

$$V(t) = V_{rest} + \frac{1}{C} \int I(t)dt$$

where $V(t)$ is the membrane potential, $I(t)$ is the input current, and C is the capacitance.

* Optical Computing: By using light instead of electrical signals to perform computations, optical computing can achieve faster processing speeds and lower energy consumption. Techniques such as photonic integrated circuits are being developed to enable high-speed data processing and transmission. The fundamental operation can be described using Maxwell's equations, which govern the behavior of electromagnetic fields.

Challenges in New Technologies

While these new paradigms offer exciting possibilities, they also come with their own set of challenges:

* Scalability: Many emerging technologies struggle with scaling from laboratory prototypes to commercially viable products. For instance, while quantum computers have shown promise in small-scale experiments, building a large-scale, fault-tolerant quantum computer remains a significant hurdle.

* Integration: The integration of new technologies with existing infrastructure poses challenges. For example, neuromorphic chips need to interface with traditional computing systems, requiring new architectures and protocols that are not yet fully developed.

* Cost: The development and manufacturing costs of novel computing technologies can be prohibitively high. As Moore's Law slows, the economic model of continuous improvement in performance per dollar is also under threat, necessitating new business models and funding strategies.

Conclusion: A Future Beyond Moore's Law

As we look to the future, it is clear that the evolution of technology beyond Moore's Law will require a multifaceted approach. The exploration of quantum, neuromorphic, and optical computing represents just a fraction of the potential pathways. The key will be to foster interdisciplinary collaboration among physicists, engineers, and computer scientists to overcome the challenges that lie ahead.

The landscape of computing is poised for transformation, driven by the need for innovation in the face of physical limitations. While Moore's Law has served as a guiding principle for decades, the next chapter in computing will likely be defined by a diverse array of technologies, each contributing uniquely to the unfolding narrative of our digital future.

In summary, while Moore's Law may be reaching its limits, the quest for advancement in computing technology is far from over. The next generation of innovations awaits, promising to redefine our relationship with technology and propel us into an era of unprecedented computational capabilities.

Forecasting the Unpredictable: What Lies Ahead

As we stand on the precipice of a new era in computing, the question looms large: what lies ahead in the world of technology? The rapid evolution of computing power, once neatly encapsulated by Moore's Law, has begun to confront the limits of silicon-based technology. This section explores the unpredictable future of computing, examining emerging paradigms, theoretical frameworks, and the challenges that accompany such advancements.

The Limits of Moore's Law

Moore's Law, which posits that the number of transistors on a microchip doubles approximately every two years, has been a guiding principle in the semiconductor industry for decades. However, as we approach the physical limits of silicon technology, the question arises: how long can this trend continue?

The fundamental equation that describes the scaling of transistors is given by:

$$N(t) = N_0 \cdot 2^{\frac{t}{T}} \tag{51}$$

where:

+ $N(t)$ is the number of transistors at time t,

+ N_0 is the initial number of transistors,

+ T is the time interval (typically two years).

As we push the boundaries of miniaturization, we encounter significant challenges, such as quantum tunneling and heat dissipation. These challenges suggest that the exponential growth predicted by Moore's Law may soon come to a halt, necessitating a shift in focus toward alternative technologies.

Emerging Technologies

With the impending limits of traditional semiconductor technology, researchers are exploring various alternatives that promise to redefine the landscape of computing. Some of the most promising technologies include:

Quantum Computing   Quantum computing leverages the principles of quantum mechanics to process information in fundamentally different ways than classical computers. Quantum bits, or qubits, can exist in multiple states simultaneously, allowing for exponentially greater computational power. The theoretical speedup of quantum algorithms, such as Shor's algorithm for factoring large numbers, can be expressed as:

$$T_{quantum} = O(n^2) \quad \text{(for factoring)} \tag{52}$$

compared to the classical $O(n^3)$ complexity. This capability could revolutionize fields such as cryptography, optimization, and material science.

Neuromorphic Computing   Inspired by the human brain, neuromorphic computing utilizes artificial neural networks to process information in a highly parallel and energy-efficient manner. The architecture of neuromorphic chips mimics the synaptic connections in the brain, leading to significant improvements in machine learning and artificial intelligence applications. The efficiency of these systems can be described by the following relationship:

$$E_{neuromorphic} \propto \frac{1}{N_{neurons} \cdot T_{processing}} \tag{53}$$

where $E_{neuromorphic}$ represents the energy consumption, $N_{neurons}$ is the number of artificial neurons, and $T_{processing}$ is the time taken for processing.

DNA Computing   DNA computing utilizes the unique properties of DNA molecules to perform complex calculations. By encoding information in the sequences of nucleotides, researchers can leverage the massive parallelism of biochemical reactions. An example of a DNA computing operation can be represented as:

$$C = \sum_{i=1}^{N} f(D_i) \tag{54}$$

where C is the computed result, D_i represents the DNA strands, and f is the function applied to each strand. This method holds potential for solving problems that are currently intractable for classical computers.

Theoretical Challenges

While these emerging technologies offer exciting possibilities, they also present a host of theoretical and practical challenges. For instance, quantum computing faces issues related to error rates and qubit coherence times, which must be addressed before widespread adoption can occur. Neuromorphic computing, while promising, still struggles with the complexity of training neural networks and ensuring scalability.

Moreover, the integration of these new technologies into existing infrastructure poses significant hurdles. The transition from classical to quantum or neuromorphic computing will require not only new hardware but also new algorithms, programming languages, and paradigms of thought.

Ethical Considerations

As we forge ahead into this unpredictable future, ethical considerations must also be at the forefront of our discussions. The deployment of advanced technologies, particularly in areas such as artificial intelligence and genetic manipulation, raises questions about privacy, security, and the potential for misuse. The balance between innovation and responsibility will be crucial in shaping a future that benefits humanity.

Conclusion

In conclusion, while the future of computing is rife with uncertainty, it also brims with potential. As we move beyond the confines of Moore's Law, the exploration of quantum, neuromorphic, and DNA computing offers a glimpse into a world where the limits of technology are continually redefined. The challenges we face are significant, but with them comes the opportunity to innovate in ways we have yet to imagine. The unpredictable nature of technological advancement is not just a challenge; it is an invitation to dream bigger and reach further into the unknown.

As we look ahead, it is imperative that we embrace this unpredictability, fostering a culture of innovation that prioritizes ethical considerations and the betterment of society. The future of computing is not just about faster processors or more efficient algorithms; it is about harnessing the power of technology to create a better world for all.

Embracing the New Era of Computing

As we stand on the precipice of a new era in computing, it is essential to reflect on the foundational principles laid out by pioneers like Gordon Moore. Moore's Law, which posits that the number of transistors on a microchip doubles approximately every two years, has driven the exponential growth of computing power. However, as we approach the physical limits of silicon-based technology, the industry must pivot towards innovative paradigms that promise to redefine the landscape of computing.

The Shift from Classical to Quantum Computing

One of the most significant advancements in recent years is the emergence of quantum computing. Unlike classical computers, which rely on bits as the smallest unit of data, quantum computers utilize quantum bits or qubits. Qubits can exist in multiple states simultaneously, thanks to the principles of superposition and entanglement. This capability allows quantum computers to perform complex calculations at unprecedented speeds.

The fundamental equation governing the behavior of qubits is derived from quantum mechanics, represented by the state vector:

$$|\psi\rangle = \alpha|0\rangle + \beta|1\rangle$$

where $|\psi\rangle$ is the state of the qubit, and α and β are complex numbers that represent the probability amplitudes of the qubit being in state $|0\rangle$ or $|1\rangle$, respectively. The probabilities of measuring the qubit in either state are given by $|\alpha|^2$ and $|\beta|^2$, satisfying the normalization condition:

$$|\alpha|^2 + |\beta|^2 = 1$$

This inherent parallelism allows quantum computers to tackle problems that are currently intractable for classical machines, such as factoring large integers, simulating quantum systems, and optimizing complex networks.

Challenges and Limitations of Quantum Computing

Despite the promise of quantum computing, several challenges must be addressed before it can be fully realized. One major issue is decoherence, which occurs when qubits lose their quantum state due to interactions with their environment. This phenomenon can lead to errors in calculations and requires robust error correction methods to maintain computational integrity.

Additionally, the development of scalable quantum hardware is still in its infancy. Current quantum processors, such as those developed by IBM and Google, have a limited number of qubits and are often susceptible to noise. Researchers are actively exploring various qubit implementations, including superconducting circuits, trapped ions, and topological qubits, each with its advantages and drawbacks.

The Role of Artificial Intelligence and Machine Learning

As we embrace this new era of computing, the integration of artificial intelligence (AI) and machine learning (ML) will play a pivotal role. AI algorithms are already being used to optimize quantum circuits, identify patterns in large datasets, and enhance data processing capabilities. The synergy between quantum computing and AI has the potential to unlock new frontiers in various fields, including healthcare, finance, and climate modeling.

For instance, in drug discovery, quantum computing can simulate molecular interactions at a level of detail unattainable by classical methods, significantly reducing the time and cost associated with bringing new drugs to market. The equation governing the energy levels of quantum systems, known as the Schrödinger equation, can be expressed as:

$$i\hbar\frac{\partial}{\partial t}|\psi(t)\rangle = \hat{H}|\psi(t)\rangle$$

where $\hat{H}$ is the Hamiltonian operator representing the total energy of the system. By solving this equation, researchers can gain insights into molecular behavior, paving the way for breakthroughs in medicine.

The Future of Computing: A Multidisciplinary Approach

Looking ahead, the future of computing will likely be characterized by a multidisciplinary approach that combines quantum computing, AI, and advanced materials science. Innovations in materials, such as graphene and other two-dimensional materials, hold promise for developing faster and more efficient transistors, potentially extending Moore's Law into new realms.

Furthermore, the rise of neuromorphic computing, which mimics the neural architecture of the human brain, offers another avenue for enhancing computational capabilities. Neuromorphic systems can process information in a manner similar to biological neurons, enabling faster and more efficient data processing. The equations governing neural networks, such as the perceptron learning rule, can be represented as:

$$w_i^{(t+1)} = w_i^{(t)} + \eta(d - y)x_i$$

where w_i are the weights, η is the learning rate, d is the desired output, y is the actual output, and x_i are the inputs. This adaptability allows neuromorphic systems to learn and evolve, much like the human brain.

Conclusion: Embracing the Unknown

In conclusion, as we embrace this new era of computing, we must remain open to the unknown possibilities that lie ahead. The convergence of quantum computing, AI, and advanced materials will undoubtedly lead to innovations that we can scarcely imagine today. As we forge this path, the legacy of visionaries like Gordon Moore will continue to inspire future generations of technologists and thinkers, driving us towards a future where computing transcends current limitations and reshapes our understanding of the world.

The journey is just beginning, and as we navigate this uncharted territory, we must remain committed to ethical considerations and the responsible development of technology, ensuring that the advancements we make benefit all of humanity.

Appendix

Key Figures in Moore's Life and Career

Robert Noyce: The Other Intel Founder

Robert Noyce, often overshadowed by his more famous counterpart, Gordon Moore, was a pivotal figure in the creation of Intel and the semiconductor industry. Born on December 12, 1927, in Burlington, Iowa, Noyce's early life was marked by a combination of academic brilliance and a natural inclination toward innovation. His journey from a small-town boy to a co-founder of one of the most influential technology companies in the world is a testament to his visionary thinking and engineering prowess.

The Early Years and Education

Noyce's fascination with technology began at a young age. He was an inquisitive child, often dismantling household gadgets to understand how they worked. This curiosity was nurtured by his family, particularly his father, a Congregational minister who encouraged intellectual exploration. Noyce attended Grinnell College in Iowa, where he earned a Bachelor of Science degree in Physics in 1949. His academic journey continued at the Massachusetts Institute of Technology (MIT), where he completed his Ph.D. in Physics in 1953. At MIT, he conducted research on the properties of semiconductors, laying the groundwork for his future innovations.

The Birth of the Integrated Circuit

Noyce's most significant contribution to the field of electronics was his invention of the integrated circuit, a groundbreaking development that would revolutionize the technology industry. In 1959, while working at Fairchild Semiconductor, he devised a method to etch multiple electronic components onto a single piece of silicon. This innovation not only reduced the size and cost of electronic devices but also significantly increased their reliability.

The equation governing the performance of an integrated circuit can be represented as:

$$R = \frac{V^2}{P} \tag{55}$$

where R is the reliability, V is the voltage, and P is the power consumption. Noyce's work directly impacted this equation, as the integrated circuit enabled devices to operate at lower power levels while maintaining high performance.

Founding Intel

In 1968, Noyce, along with Gordon Moore and a group of engineers, founded Intel Corporation. The partnership between Noyce and Moore was synergistic; while Moore brought his analytical mind and vision for scaling technology, Noyce contributed his practical engineering skills and innovative spirit. Their complementary strengths were crucial in navigating the challenges of establishing a new company in a rapidly evolving industry.

Intel's first product, the 3101 Schottky bipolar random-access memory (RAM), was released in 1969. However, it was the launch of the Intel 4004 microprocessor in 1971 that marked a turning point for the company and the industry. The 4004 was the first commercially available microprocessor, integrating the functions of a computer's central processing unit (CPU) onto a single chip. This innovation laid the foundation for the personal computing revolution.

Noyce's Leadership Style

Noyce's leadership style was characterized by openness and collaboration. He believed in fostering a culture of innovation, encouraging his team to take risks and explore new ideas. This approach not only cultivated creativity but also established Intel as a leader in technological advancement. Noyce's management philosophy can be summarized by the following principles:

- **Empowerment:** Noyce empowered his employees to make decisions and take ownership of their projects.

- **Innovation:** He promoted an environment where experimentation and innovation were valued.

+ **Collaboration:** Noyce emphasized teamwork and collaboration, recognizing that diverse perspectives lead to better solutions.

Legacy and Impact

Robert Noyce's legacy extends far beyond his contributions to Intel. His work on the integrated circuit has had a lasting impact on the entire electronics industry. The principles of miniaturization and integration that he championed continue to drive technological advancements today.

Noyce's influence can be seen in the exponential growth of computing power over the decades, often summarized by Moore's Law, which states that the number of transistors on a microchip doubles approximately every two years. This phenomenon is not only a testament to Moore's vision but also to the foundational work laid by Noyce in the development of the integrated circuit.

In recognition of his contributions, Noyce received numerous awards throughout his career, including the National Medal of Technology and Innovation in 1987. His induction into the National Inventors Hall of Fame in 2000 further solidified his status as a pioneer in the field of electronics.

Conclusion

In summary, Robert Noyce was more than just the other co-founder of Intel; he was a visionary whose innovations transformed the landscape of technology. His work on the integrated circuit set the stage for the digital age, and his leadership style fostered an environment where innovation could flourish. As we reflect on the history of computing, it is essential to recognize Noyce's contributions and the profound impact he had on the industry. The legacy of Robert Noyce continues to inspire future generations of engineers and innovators, reminding us that curiosity, collaboration, and creativity are the cornerstones of technological advancement.

Andy Grove: The Protege Becomes the Leader

Andy Grove, born András István Gróf in Budapest, Hungary, in 1936, is often regarded as one of the most influential figures in the semiconductor industry and a pivotal leader in Intel's ascent to dominance. His journey from a war-torn Europe to the helm of one of the world's most powerful technology companies is not only a tale of personal triumph but also a testament to the power of vision, resilience, and innovation.

Early Life and Education

Grove's early life was marked by adversity. He fled Hungary during the 1956 revolution, arriving in the United States with little more than a dream and a determination to succeed. His academic journey began at City College of New York, where he earned a degree in Chemical Engineering. He later pursued a Ph.D. at the University of California, Berkeley, where his research focused on the chemical properties of silicon, laying the groundwork for his future contributions to the semiconductor industry.

Joining Intel

In 1968, Grove joined Intel, a fledgling company co-founded by Gordon Moore and Robert Noyce. At Intel, he quickly distinguished himself as a brilliant engineer and a strategic thinker. His expertise in chemical engineering and his understanding of semiconductor manufacturing processes positioned him as a key player in the company's growth.

Grove's ascent within Intel was meteoric. By 1979, he had become the company's president, and in 1987, he took over as CEO. His leadership style was characterized by a hands-on approach and a relentless focus on execution. He famously coined the phrase, "Only the paranoid survive," which encapsulated his belief that constant vigilance and adaptability were essential for success in the rapidly evolving tech landscape.

Leadership Philosophy

Grove's management philosophy was rooted in the concept of "high output management." He emphasized the importance of measuring performance, setting clear goals, and fostering a culture of accountability. This approach not only drove efficiency but also encouraged innovation within the organization. Under his leadership, Intel introduced several groundbreaking products, including the 286, 386, and Pentium microprocessors, which revolutionized personal computing.

$$\text{Output} = \text{Throughput} \times \text{Efficiency} \tag{56}$$

This equation reflects Grove's belief that maximizing output required not only increasing throughput but also ensuring that the processes were efficient. He implemented rigorous performance metrics and encouraged employees to embrace data-driven decision-making.

Navigating Challenges

Grove's tenure at Intel was not without challenges. The company faced significant competition from Japanese manufacturers in the 1980s, which threatened its market share. In response, Grove led a strategic shift towards a focus on microprocessors, a decision that would ultimately pay off. He championed the idea of "strategic inflection points," moments when a company must adapt to survive and thrive in changing market conditions.

Grove's ability to foresee industry trends was remarkable. He recognized the potential of personal computing early on and positioned Intel as a leader in this burgeoning market. His foresight and decisive action during critical moments helped Intel not only to survive but to flourish.

The Legacy of Andy Grove

Grove's legacy at Intel is profound. He transformed the company from a memory chip manufacturer into a dominant force in the microprocessor market. His leadership style and management principles have been studied and emulated by countless business leaders worldwide.

In recognition of his contributions, Grove received numerous accolades throughout his career, including the National Medal of Technology and Innovation in 2000. His influence extended beyond Intel; he became a respected voice in the tech industry, advocating for innovation and ethical leadership.

Conclusion

Andy Grove's journey from a refugee to a titan of the tech industry exemplifies the power of vision, resilience, and strategic thinking. His partnership with Gordon Moore not only shaped Intel's trajectory but also left an indelible mark on the technology landscape. As the protégé who became a leader, Grove's story is a testament to the impact of strong leadership in driving innovation and success in an ever-evolving industry.

In summary, Andy Grove's legacy is not merely one of corporate success; it is a blueprint for future generations of leaders in technology and beyond. His insights into management and strategy continue to inspire and guide those who seek to navigate the complexities of the modern business world.

Steve Jobs: A Complex Relationship with the Apple Co-Founder

The relationship between Gordon Moore and Steve Jobs is emblematic of the intricate web of collaboration and rivalry that defines the tech industry. While both figures are giants in their respective domains, their paths crossed in ways that highlighted both synergy and tension, ultimately shaping the trajectory of modern computing.

The Early Encounters

Moore and Jobs first encountered one another in the burgeoning world of Silicon Valley, where innovation was the currency of success. In the early 1980s, as Jobs was busy crafting the Apple II and later the Macintosh, Moore was entrenched in the development of Intel's microprocessors. The Apple II, with its user-friendly interface and robust software ecosystem, was revolutionizing personal computing, while Intel was providing the raw computational power behind these innovations.

The partnership between hardware and software was critical during this era. Intel's microprocessors, particularly the 8088, powered the original IBM PC, which in turn laid the groundwork for the personal computer revolution. Jobs, recognizing the importance of powerful yet accessible computing, sought to create machines that not only performed well but also appealed to the aesthetic sensibilities of consumers. This focus on design and user experience would become a hallmark of Apple's identity.

The Competitive Landscape

Despite their shared interests in advancing technology, the relationship between Moore and Jobs was not without its competitive tensions. The introduction of the Macintosh in 1984 marked a significant moment in computing history, positioning Apple as a formidable competitor to Intel's primary clients, including IBM. Jobs' vision for a user-friendly operating system and integrated hardware created a direct challenge to the traditional computing paradigms that Intel had supported.

Moore, on the other hand, was focused on the relentless pace of innovation that defined Moore's Law, which posits that the number of transistors on a microchip doubles approximately every two years, leading to exponential increases in performance. This principle not only fueled Intel's growth but also became a foundational element in the evolution of personal computing. Jobs, while initially benefiting from Intel's advancements, began to carve out a niche that emphasized a closed ecosystem, contrasting sharply with Intel's open architecture approach.

Philosophical Differences

At the heart of their complex relationship were fundamental philosophical differences. Moore embodied the engineer's mindset—focused on the technical specifications, performance metrics, and the relentless pursuit of advancement through innovation. Jobs, in contrast, was a visionary who prioritized the user experience, design aesthetics, and the emotional connection that technology could foster with its users.

This divergence was starkly illustrated during the development of the Macintosh. Jobs' insistence on a graphical user interface (GUI) and the mouse as a primary input device was revolutionary, but it also placed significant demands on Intel's engineering capabilities. While Moore's team was adept at pushing the boundaries of microprocessor technology, they were less inclined to prioritize the integration of hardware and software in the way that Jobs envisioned.

Collaboration and Conflict

Despite these differences, there were moments of collaboration. Intel's technology was integral to Apple's success, and Jobs often spoke highly of the contributions made by Intel in powering his machines. However, as Apple grew, so did its desire to control its own destiny. The introduction of the PowerPC architecture in the early 1990s marked a significant departure from Intel's x86 architecture, further complicating their relationship.

Jobs' departure from Apple in 1985 also shifted the dynamics. During his time away from the company, he founded NeXT, a company that aimed to create high-end workstations for higher education and business markets. NeXT's reliance on advanced technology and its focus on software development highlighted the ongoing evolution of computing paradigms. Moore, still at the helm of Intel, continued to push the boundaries of microprocessor technology, but the competition with Apple became more pronounced.

The Resurgence of Apple

Upon Jobs' return to Apple in 1997, the landscape had changed dramatically. Apple was struggling, and the introduction of the iMac in 1998 marked a pivotal moment in its resurgence. The iMac's innovative design and integrated components were a testament to Jobs' vision, but they also relied heavily on Intel's advancements in microprocessor technology. The partnership between Apple and Intel, which began in earnest in the early 2000s, transformed the computing landscape once again.

This collaboration signified a reconciliation of sorts, as both companies recognized the value of their respective strengths. Intel's processors powered Apple's new generation of products, including the MacBook and the Mac Pro, while Apple's design ethos and software innovations helped to revitalize Intel's market presence.

The Legacy of Their Relationship

The relationship between Moore and Jobs serves as a case study in the interplay of competition and collaboration within the tech industry. Their interactions exemplified the tension between engineering excellence and visionary design. While they often operated in parallel tracks, their legacies are intertwined in the story of computing.

Moore's Law continues to drive innovation in microprocessor technology, while Jobs' emphasis on design and user experience has shaped the way technology is perceived and consumed. Together, they have left an indelible mark on the industry, illustrating that progress often arises from a complex interplay of ideas, philosophies, and personalities.

In conclusion, the relationship between Gordon Moore and Steve Jobs is a testament to the dynamic nature of the tech world. Their paths, while sometimes divergent, ultimately converged in ways that propelled the industry forward. Understanding this relationship not only sheds light on their individual contributions but also highlights the collaborative spirit that continues to drive innovation in technology today.

$$\text{Moore's Law: } N(t) = N_0 \cdot 2^{\frac{t}{T}} \tag{57}$$

where $N(t)$ is the number of transistors at time t, N_0 is the initial number of transistors, and T is the time period over which the doubling occurs.

The equation encapsulates the essence of the rapid technological advancement that both Moore and Jobs championed, demonstrating that innovation is not merely a product of individual brilliance but rather a confluence of ideas, vision, and relentless pursuit of excellence.

Influential Partnerships and Collaborations

Gordon Moore's journey through the semiconductor landscape was not a solitary endeavor; rather, it was marked by a series of influential partnerships and collaborations that shaped the trajectory of Intel and the technology industry at large. These relationships were pivotal in fostering innovation, driving technological advancements, and navigating the complexities of a rapidly evolving market.

Robert Noyce: The Co-Founder and Visionary

One of the most significant partnerships in Moore's career was with Robert Noyce, co-founder of Intel and a pioneering figure in the semiconductor industry. Noyce, known for his invention of the integrated circuit, complemented Moore's analytical prowess with his visionary thinking and entrepreneurial spirit. Their collaboration was characterized by a shared commitment to innovation and a deep understanding of the technological landscape.

The synergy between Moore and Noyce can be illustrated through the development of the first microprocessor, the Intel 4004. This groundbreaking product was the result of their combined expertise, with Moore's insights into semiconductor physics and Noyce's ability to envision the market potential of such technology. The partnership allowed Intel to not only lead the industry but also to redefine it.

Andy Grove: The Protege Becomes the Leader

Another crucial figure in Moore's narrative is Andy Grove, who joined Intel in its early days and eventually rose to become its CEO. Grove's relationship with Moore was one of mentorship and mutual respect. As Moore's protégé, Grove learned the intricacies of management and innovation, eventually shaping Intel's corporate culture and operational strategies.

Grove's management philosophy, which emphasized rigorous performance metrics and a relentless focus on execution, was deeply influenced by Moore's vision. The partnership between them is best exemplified by the introduction of the "copy exactly" manufacturing process, which ensured consistent quality across Intel's production lines. This principle became a cornerstone of Intel's operational excellence and competitive advantage.

Collaboration with Academia: Bridging Theory and Practice

Moore's partnerships extended beyond the corporate realm, reaching into academia where he sought to bridge the gap between theoretical research and practical application. Collaborations with renowned institutions such as Stanford University and UC Berkeley allowed Moore to tap into cutting-edge research while also providing a platform for students and researchers to engage with the industry.

For instance, the partnership with Stanford led to the development of advanced semiconductor materials and fabrication techniques, which were crucial for the evolution of microprocessors. Moore's commitment to fostering these academic collaborations not only enhanced Intel's technological capabilities but also contributed to the growth of the semiconductor field as a whole.

Strategic Alliances and Joint Ventures

In addition to individual partnerships, Moore recognized the importance of strategic alliances and joint ventures in expanding Intel's market reach and technological prowess. Collaborations with companies such as Microsoft and IBM were instrumental in establishing the PC ecosystem, which propelled Intel to the forefront of the personal computing revolution.

The alliance with Microsoft, in particular, was a game-changer. By working together to optimize software and hardware compatibility, Intel and Microsoft created a seamless user experience that drove the adoption of personal computers. This partnership exemplified the principle of co-innovation, where both companies leveraged their strengths to create a dominant market position.

Global Collaborations: Navigating International Markets

As Intel expanded globally, Moore's ability to forge partnerships with international firms became increasingly important. Collaborations with companies in Japan, Europe, and emerging markets allowed Intel to adapt its products to diverse consumer needs and regulatory environments.

For example, partnerships with Japanese manufacturers facilitated the transfer of advanced manufacturing techniques, significantly enhancing Intel's production capabilities. These global collaborations not only solidified Intel's position as a market leader but also highlighted Moore's understanding of the interconnectedness of the global technology landscape.

Conclusion: The Power of Collaboration

In summary, the influential partnerships and collaborations throughout Gordon Moore's career were instrumental in shaping not only Intel's success but also the broader semiconductor industry. From his early days with Robert Noyce to his mentorship of Andy Grove and strategic alliances with key players in the tech ecosystem, Moore's collaborative approach underscored the importance of teamwork in driving innovation.

These relationships exemplify the notion that no great achievement is made in isolation; rather, it is through collaboration that groundbreaking ideas are born and realized. As Moore's legacy continues to influence future generations, the lessons learned from his partnerships serve as a reminder of the power of working together to push the boundaries of technology and human potential.

Timeline of Major Technological Breakthroughs

The Evolution of Semiconductors

The evolution of semiconductors is a cornerstone of modern electronics, driving the development of everything from the simplest transistors to the most complex microprocessors. This section explores the key milestones in the history of semiconductors, their underlying theories, and the challenges faced along the way.

1. The Birth of Semiconductors

The concept of semiconductors emerged in the early 20th century when scientists began to understand the electrical properties of materials. Unlike conductors, which allow electricity to flow freely, and insulators, which block it, semiconductors exhibit a unique behavior: their conductivity can be manipulated by introducing impurities, a process known as doping.

The first significant discovery was made in 1904 when John Ambrose Fleming invented the vacuum tube, which used thermionic emission to control electron flow. However, vacuum tubes were bulky and inefficient, leading researchers to seek alternatives.

2. The Discovery of the Transistor

The true revolution in semiconductor technology began with the invention of the transistor in 1947 by John Bardeen, Walter Brattain, and William Shockley at Bell Labs. The transistor, a solid-state device, allowed for the amplification and switching of electrical signals without the need for a vacuum tube.

The basic structure of a transistor consists of three layers of semiconductor material, typically silicon, doped to create regions of positive (p-type) and negative (n-type) charge carriers. The operation of a transistor can be described using the following equation for current flow:

$$I_C = \beta I_B \qquad (58)$$

where I_C is the collector current, I_B is the base current, and β (beta) is the current gain of the transistor.

This invention laid the groundwork for the development of integrated circuits and microprocessors, leading to the miniaturization of electronic devices.

3. The Integrated Circuit Revolution

In 1958, Jack Kilby of Texas Instruments and Robert Noyce of Fairchild Semiconductor independently developed the integrated circuit (IC), which combined multiple transistors and components onto a single chip of semiconductor material. This innovation drastically reduced the size and cost of electronic devices while increasing reliability.

The key equation governing the operation of integrated circuits is the relationship between voltage, current, and resistance, expressed by Ohm's Law:

$$V = IR \tag{59}$$

where V is voltage, I is current, and R is resistance. This relationship is fundamental to understanding circuit design and functionality.

4. Advancements in Semiconductor Materials

The 1970s and 1980s saw significant advancements in semiconductor materials beyond silicon. Gallium arsenide (GaAs) became popular for high-frequency applications due to its superior electron mobility compared to silicon. Additionally, the development of compound semiconductors enabled the creation of light-emitting diodes (LEDs) and laser diodes, revolutionizing the display and communication industries.

The bandgap energy of a semiconductor material is crucial in determining its electrical properties. The bandgap E_g can be expressed as:

$$E_g = E_c - E_v \tag{60}$$

where E_c is the energy of the conduction band and E_v is the energy of the valence band. This property influences the absorption and emission of light in optoelectronic devices.

5. The Era of Microprocessors

The introduction of the microprocessor in the early 1970s marked a significant turning point in the evolution of semiconductors. The Intel 4004, released in 1971, was the first commercially available microprocessor, integrating the functions of a computer's central processing unit (CPU) onto a single chip. This innovation paved the way for personal computers and the digital age.

The performance of microprocessors can be described using the following equation for processing speed:

$$\text{MIPS} = \frac{\text{Clock Speed (MHz)}}{\text{Cycles per Instruction}} \tag{61}$$

where MIPS stands for Million Instructions Per Second. This metric allows for the comparison of processing power across different microprocessor architectures.

6. Challenges and Future Directions

Despite the successes of semiconductor technology, challenges remain. As transistors continue to shrink in size, approaching the atomic scale, issues such as quantum tunneling and heat dissipation become increasingly significant.

The semiconductor industry is now exploring new materials, such as graphene and carbon nanotubes, which promise to overcome these limitations. Furthermore, advancements in quantum computing and neuromorphic computing are set to redefine the landscape of semiconductor technology.

In conclusion, the evolution of semiconductors is a testament to human ingenuity and innovation. From the humble beginnings of the transistor to the complexities of modern microprocessors, the journey has been marked by groundbreaking discoveries and relentless pursuit of excellence. As we look to the future, the potential for semiconductor technology remains boundless, promising to shape the next generation of electronic devices and systems.

Milestones in Intel's History

Intel Corporation, founded in 1968, has been at the forefront of the semiconductor industry, driving technological advancements that have shaped the modern computing landscape. Below are key milestones that mark Intel's journey from its inception to its status as a global leader in microprocessor technology.

1968: The Birth of Intel

Intel was founded by Robert Noyce and Gordon Moore, who sought to create a company focused on semiconductor memory products. The name "Intel" is derived from "Integrated Electronics." This marked the beginning of a new era in computing, where integrated circuits would replace discrete components.

1971: The First Microprocessor - Intel 4004

In 1971, Intel introduced the 4004, the world's first commercially available microprocessor. It was a 4-bit CPU that could execute approximately 92,000 instructions per second. The 4004 was revolutionary because it integrated all the components of a computer's central processing unit (CPU) onto a single chip, paving the way for the development of personal computers.

$$\text{Clock Speed} = \frac{\text{Number of Instructions}}{\text{Time}} \tag{62}$$

The 4004's architecture consisted of a 4-bit data bus, a 12-bit address bus, and a set of registers, allowing it to address up to 4 KB of memory. This innovation set the stage for future microprocessor developments.

1972: Introduction of the 8008

Building on the success of the 4004, Intel released the 8008 in 1972, which was an 8-bit microprocessor capable of addressing 16 KB of memory. It was used in early computer systems, including the first commercial personal computer, the Mark-8.

1974: The Intel 8080 and the Birth of the Personal Computer

The Intel 8080, released in 1974, was a significant advancement over its predecessors. It was a full 8-bit microprocessor and became the foundation for early personal computers. The 8080 could execute about 200,000 instructions per second and was used in systems such as the Altair 8800, which is often credited with sparking the personal computing revolution.

1982: The Intel 8086 and the x86 Architecture

The introduction of the Intel 8086 in 1978 marked a pivotal moment in computing history, as it introduced the x86 architecture, which would become the basis for most personal computers. The 8086 featured a 16-bit architecture and was capable of addressing up to 1 MB of memory. This architecture laid the groundwork for future Intel processors and established a standard for compatibility in the PC industry.

Addressable Memory $= 2^n$ bytes, where n is the number of address bits   (63)

1985: The 80386 and the Era of 32-Bit Computing

The 80386, released in 1985, was Intel's first 32-bit microprocessor. It introduced virtual memory management and improved multitasking capabilities, allowing multiple applications to run simultaneously without interference. This marked a significant leap in computing power and efficiency.

1993: The Pentium Processor

The launch of the Pentium processor in 1993 was a watershed moment for Intel. It featured superscalar architecture, allowing it to execute multiple instructions per clock cycle. The Pentium's performance improvements and multimedia capabilities made it the de facto standard for personal computers throughout the 1990s.

$$\text{Performance} = \text{Clock Speed} \times \text{Instructions per Cycle} \qquad (64)$$

1997: The Pentium II and the Rise of Multimedia

The Pentium II, introduced in 1997, further enhanced multimedia performance with the addition of MMX technology, which allowed for improved processing of graphics and sound. This was crucial for the growing demand for multimedia applications in personal computing.

2006: The Core Microarchitecture

Intel's introduction of the Core microarchitecture in 2006 marked a shift towards energy efficiency and performance. The Core Duo and Core 2 Duo processors provided significant performance improvements while consuming less power, catering to the growing mobile computing market.

2011: The Second Generation Intel Core Processors

The launch of the second-generation Intel Core processors, codenamed "Sandy Bridge," introduced integrated graphics and improved performance per watt. This innovation allowed for more powerful laptops and desktops that could handle demanding applications without excessive heat generation.

2019: The 10th Generation Intel Core Processors

Intel's 10th generation Core processors, known as "Comet Lake," continued to push the boundaries of performance and efficiency. These processors introduced features such as Thunderbolt 3 support and enhanced AI capabilities, further solidifying Intel's position in the competitive CPU market.

2021: The Introduction of the 11th Generation Core Processors

Intel's 11th generation Core processors, codenamed "Tiger Lake," utilized a new 10nm SuperFin technology, offering significant improvements in performance and power efficiency. These processors were designed to meet the demands of modern workloads, including AI and machine learning applications.

Conclusion

Intel's journey from a small startup to a global powerhouse in the semiconductor industry is marked by a series of groundbreaking innovations. Each milestone has contributed to the evolution of computing, shaping the technology we rely on today. As Intel continues to innovate, the legacy of its past achievements serves as a foundation for future advancements in computing technology.

The Impact of Moore's Law on Computing

Gordon Moore's prediction, famously articulated in 1965, posited that the number of transistors on a microchip would double approximately every two years, leading to an exponential increase in computing power while simultaneously reducing costs. This observation, now known as **Moore's Law**, has profoundly influenced the trajectory of the semiconductor industry and the broader field of computing.

Theoretical Foundation

The essence of Moore's Law lies in the principles of semiconductor physics and integrated circuit design. The exponential growth in transistor density can be described mathematically by the equation:

$$N(t) = N_0 \cdot 2^{\frac{t}{T}} \tag{65}$$

where:

+ $N(t)$ is the number of transistors at time t,

+ N_0 is the initial number of transistors,

+ T is the doubling time (approximately 2 years).

This equation illustrates how the ability to miniaturize components and enhance fabrication techniques has led to a dramatic increase in the number of transistors that can be placed on a single chip, effectively boosting computational capabilities.

Technological Advancements

The implications of Moore's Law have been vast, driving advancements in various domains of computing. For instance, the transition from the Intel 4004, which had 2,300 transistors, to the Intel Core i7, which boasts over 1.7 billion transistors, exemplifies this exponential growth. This increase has enabled the development of more complex and capable processors, facilitating innovations in artificial intelligence, machine learning, and data processing.

Challenges and Limitations

Despite its historical accuracy, Moore's Law faces challenges in contemporary computing. As transistors approach atomic scales, issues such as **quantum tunneling** and **heat dissipation** become significant hurdles. The physical limitations of silicon-based technologies prompt the exploration of alternative materials and architectures, such as:

- **Graphene and Carbon Nanotubes:** These materials promise higher electron mobility and lower power consumption.

- **Quantum Computing:** This emerging field aims to leverage quantum bits (qubits) for exponentially faster computations, challenging traditional binary processing.

Real-World Examples

The impact of Moore's Law extends beyond theoretical discussions, manifesting in tangible advancements across industries. For example:

- **Smartphones:** The rapid evolution of mobile technology, driven by Moore's Law, has transformed smartphones into powerful computing devices, enabling applications ranging from augmented reality to real-time data analytics.

- **Cloud Computing:** The exponential increase in processing power has facilitated the rise of cloud services, allowing businesses to harness vast computational resources without the need for extensive local infrastructure.

+ **Artificial Intelligence:** The ability to process large datasets quickly has accelerated advancements in AI, enabling applications such as natural language processing and image recognition.

The Future Beyond Moore's Law

As we move further into the 21st century, the relevance of Moore's Law is being re-evaluated. While the law has served as a guiding principle for decades, the industry is now exploring new paradigms for computing. Technologies such as neuromorphic computing, which mimics the neural structures of the human brain, and advancements in software optimization are paving the way for the next generation of computational capabilities.

$$P = \frac{E}{t} \tag{66}$$

This equation, where P represents power, E is energy, and t is time, highlights the importance of energy efficiency in future computing systems. As we approach the limits of traditional scaling, the focus is shifting towards maximizing performance per watt rather than sheer transistor counts.

Conclusion

In summary, Moore's Law has been a cornerstone of the computing revolution, driving innovation and shaping the technological landscape. While it faces challenges, its legacy continues to influence research and development in the semiconductor industry and beyond. The quest for new computing paradigms will ensure that the spirit of Moore's vision lives on, guiding future advancements in technology and reshaping our world.

Key Technological Advancements and Discoveries

The journey of technology, particularly in the realm of computing and semiconductors, has been marked by groundbreaking advancements and discoveries that have fundamentally transformed our world. This section delves into some of the pivotal milestones that not only shaped the trajectory of Gordon Moore's career but also revolutionized the industry as a whole.

The Transistor: A Paradigm Shift

The invention of the transistor at Bell Labs in 1947 by John Bardeen, Walter Brattain, and William Shockley is often hailed as one of the most significant technological advancements of the 20th century. The transistor, a semiconductor device used to amplify or switch electronic signals, replaced the bulky vacuum tubes and paved the way for modern electronics.

$$I_C = \beta I_B \tag{67}$$

Where I_C is the collector current, I_B is the base current, and β (beta) is the current gain of the transistor. This equation illustrates the fundamental operation of the transistor, enabling it to control larger currents with smaller ones, thus acting as a switch or amplifier.

The Integrated Circuit: Miniaturization and Efficiency

The development of the integrated circuit (IC) in the late 1950s by Jack Kilby and Robert Noyce marked another significant leap in technology. By embedding multiple transistors and other components on a single chip, ICs dramatically reduced the size and cost of electronic devices while increasing their reliability.

$$C = \frac{Q}{V} \tag{68}$$

Where C is capacitance, Q is the charge, and V is the voltage. The integration of capacitors, resistors, and transistors on a single chip allowed for the creation of complex circuits that were previously unimaginable.

Microprocessors: The Brain of Computing

The introduction of the microprocessor in the early 1970s, particularly with Intel's 4004 in 1971, revolutionized computing. This compact chip contained the functions of a CPU, allowing for the creation of personal computers and changing the landscape of technology forever.

$$T = \frac{1}{f} \tag{69}$$

Where T is the period of the clock cycle and f is the frequency. The microprocessor's ability to perform millions of calculations per second (measured in MHz and later GHz) enabled the development of sophisticated applications and systems.

Moore's Law: The Guiding Principle

Gordon Moore's observation in 1965 that the number of transistors on a chip doubles approximately every two years has been a guiding principle for the semiconductor industry. This empirical law has driven innovation and set the pace for technological advancement.

$$N(t) = N_0 \cdot 2^{\frac{t}{T}} \tag{70}$$

Where $N(t)$ is the number of transistors at time t, N_0 is the initial number of transistors, and T is the doubling time (approximately 2 years). This exponential growth has resulted in more powerful and efficient processors, enabling advancements in artificial intelligence, machine learning, and beyond.

The Rise of the Internet: Connectivity and Information Sharing

The development of the Internet in the late 20th century transformed how information is shared and accessed globally. Protocols such as TCP/IP and the advent of the World Wide Web by Tim Berners-Lee in 1989 facilitated connectivity, leading to an information revolution.

$$R = \frac{V}{I} \tag{71}$$

Where R is resistance, V is voltage, and I is current. The principles of networking and data transmission rely on these electrical fundamentals, ensuring efficient communication across vast distances.

Artificial Intelligence: The New Frontier

In recent years, advancements in artificial intelligence (AI) have begun to reshape industries and redefine the boundaries of technology. Machine learning algorithms, powered by increased computational capabilities, have led to breakthroughs in various fields, including healthcare, finance, and autonomous systems.

$$y = f(x) + \epsilon \tag{72}$$

Where y is the predicted output, $f(x)$ is the function representing the model, and ϵ is the error term. This equation captures the essence of regression analysis, a fundamental technique in machine learning, allowing systems to learn from data and make predictions.

Quantum Computing: The Next Leap

As we look to the future, quantum computing represents the next frontier in technological advancement. By leveraging the principles of quantum mechanics, quantum computers have the potential to solve complex problems that are currently intractable for classical computers.

$$|\psi\rangle = \alpha|0\rangle + \beta|1\rangle \tag{73}$$

Where $|\psi\rangle$ is the quantum state, and α and β are complex coefficients representing the probability amplitudes of the qubit being in states $|0\rangle$ or $|1\rangle$. This principle of superposition allows quantum computers to perform multiple calculations simultaneously, offering unprecedented computational power.

Conclusion

The key technological advancements and discoveries discussed in this section illustrate the remarkable journey of innovation that has defined the semiconductor and computing industries. Each milestone has built upon the previous one, creating a cascade of technological evolution that continues to shape our world. From the humble transistor to the ambitious realm of quantum computing, the legacy of these discoveries is a testament to human ingenuity and the relentless pursuit of knowledge.

Index